This World and One More

C. Roxanne Hack

WESTBOW
PRESS®
A DIVISION OF THOMAS NELSON
& ZONDERVAN

WestBow Press books may be ordered through booksellers or by contacting:

WestBow Press
A Division of Thomas Nelson & Zondervan
1663 Liberty Drive
Bloomington, IN 47403
www.westbowpress.com
844-714-3454

Cover Art Credit: Haley Hack
Author Photo Credit: Kellan Knapper

ISBN: 979-8-3850-1871-0 (sc)
ISBN: 979-8-3850-1872-7 (e)

Library of Congress Control Number: 2024902827

Print information available on the last page.

WestBow Press rev. date: 04/04/2024

Contents

Dedication

My mother, my "best bud". She was small in stature but a mighty warrior. The wars are something to be shared, but more importantly, the triumphs attributed to an overcomer who never negated gratitude and utilized the words, "Thank you Lord" more than anyone I've known. While what's contained in this book may not have been the way she desired to share her experiences and faith, she would have understood that God's ways are better than ours, and while Alzheimer's and dementia certainly attempted to take control of her life; they never took the most important entity to her, her faith in a loving and good God, and her relationship with Jesus.

My daughter, my other "best bud" and I know Mom's too. Eight years during your childhood involved experiences most children don't encounter directly or consistently. Not once did you complain or balk. God sent you to us for many reasons, one, is teaching me about life and what it truly means. I thank you for all you were to Mom. I thank you for all you were to me during one of the most difficult seasons in my life. I thank you for being strong beyond measure. My hope and prayer is that you remember the good, happy times with your grandmother as well as those times of struggles leading to your courage and perseverance. May God continue to guide you throughout your journey in life. I love you Shiloh!

My brothers and extended family. Each one of you had a special place in mom's heart. One filled with unconditional love, concern, and a desire for you to possess a personal relationship with our Creator. Thank you for loving her. Thank you for being a tactical and loving backup during this fire of life. I love you all!

Haley Hack, thank you for your contribution to this book. Grandmother would be so thankful and proud of the woman you are. Continue to be a light!

Thank You, Lord.

Preface

Growing up, it wasn't ingrained in me to be a caregiver for anyone. But then, neither was the profession of firefighting where I spent twenty years. Throughout those twenty years, I found myself engulfed with fire all around me literally and figuratively. It was not until my mother was diagnosed with Alzheimer's and dementia did I find myself preparing to fight the most challenging fire ever presented to me. This would be an eight-year journey with five of those years being under the same roof experiencing the same fires of life figuratively engulfed by the one. Many lessons were learned during this time including tactical responses as well as lessons about God, love, life, and perseverance to a higher degree. It led me to reminders of how people are put into your life for a reason and how you are never forgotten nor forsaken. It painted a picture of faith in its highest form and a confirmation that God consistently dwells among us, especially amid chaos and confusion. It taught me that yes, **JESUS** is the sweetest name on earth and one not to be forgotten no matter how the enemy tries. This challenge came with many difficulties that would include resolves found through trial and error, prayerful petitions, and a will to see it through. I share practical applications as well as topics that seemed to stand out during our journey. May "This World and One More" be an invitation to you to experience the only hope we have in this present world, a knowledge and discernment of the "One More."

One More?

"This world and one more"! I heard my mother say that phrase passed down from her mother time and time again after she heard the sad news occurring around her. The meaning behind it never clicked upon hearing it and I would venture to say that Mom took for granted that I automatically knew its connotation. I am almost ashamed to say that I never really paid too much attention. Once I did, I assumed it meant that our little circle of the world on this planet outside of the things this world offered was what she was referring to. Once she was diagnosed with Alzheimer's and dementia and I became her primary caregiver, I created my definition of the phrase. Having and living with someone who has been diagnosed with these diseases creates another world outside of the one we once knew. It was only during our journey together that I finally realized the true meaning of "This World and One More" and the one which she knew it to have.

Everything bad that happens on this planet is a result of our fallen world. God does not set out to harm us. **"For He does not willingly bring affliction or grief to anyone." Lamentations 3:33 (NIV)** What He does do though is promise His children eternal life after we leave this earth. Ding ding, light bulb episode! The "one more"! The world to which we are promised after leaving this earth. The very reason mom would constantly repeat that phrase. I truly grasp now the hope in the world we are promised after we leave this world is one to repeatedly acknowledge during the life we live on this earth with all its trials, tribulations, and sorrows. I will continue her legacy by including "This World and One More" in my vocabulary not only to memorialize her but to serve as a reminder that everything that happens to us, all the filth, ugliness, sorrow, grief, etc. is only temporary. The moment we exit our journey on earth is when true peace begins. It is a daunting task to face the lessons presented to us by God through our hardships and sufferings. As life continues and we survive yet another tribulation, we are reminded of His faithfulness and must be willing to recognize the lessons found in each.

After a diagnosis that lasted eight years and living together for five of them, and as much as I have witnessed in my experiences in life, I would never have seen the lesson in dealing with the diseases of Alzheimer's and dementia. If you are experiencing it right now, believe me, I found valuable information during our journey, much through trial and error, but also stumbling on what God wanted me to learn. This information helped me hang on and take things a day at a time. I realized that turning those diseases around to find the good, which was a task in and of itself, was a turning point in my acceptance of it. I always told Mom we were not going down without a fight and I eventually found out that what the enemy intends for harm, God uses it for good. (**Genesis 50:20 - NIV**). One of the first lessons taught by these diseases is to live in the moment. That's how those stricken with it live. Forget the past as they tend to do. It is a reiteration of Isaiah 43:18, "**Forget the former things; do not dwell on the past.** Do not look into the future because we truly don't know what tomorrow holds. Live for the moment! Enjoy the moments you have every day and don't take them for granted. The next lesson is truly divine intervention for me. I always believed that no amount of theology could make me believe in God and the sacrifice made through Jesus more than seeing it lived throughout my mother's life and this belief continued during our journey with the diseases. You see, my mother's memory failed but the one constant presence in her heart and mind, the One who continued to stay in her memory despite the loss of much was that of Jesus and the love God has for each of us. She never forgot that. It is indeed a mystery; or is it?

It was a reiteration of her life's theme and one which she held deep in her heart. It's something that will stay with me for the rest of my life.

Whether you are a Christian or not, this is a small version of our story, our love story, and it could not be experienced or written about without the only hope mom would ever cling to. The hope of an everlasting peace that surpasses all understanding. The hope in another world. I pray you find peace amid suffering, joy in the midst of grief, happiness amid sadness and direction in the midst of a life being scattered, looking forward to a world with no more pain, memory loss, repetition, or suffering, and with complete wholeness.

"Joy"ce Meyers Hack

✝

Joyce Meyers Hack was bigger than life but in a humble sort of way. She loved with her whole heart. She hurt with her whole heart. To provide you with a condensed version, Mom was born in a single parent environment, raised by a mother who loved and cared for her deeply and neglected by a father who had many issues of his own. While her mother could quote scripture, she only attended church when my mother was baptized. Mom was introduced to Jesus through her family's landlord who eventually became a beloved friend. She witnessed multiple relationships in her mother's life. She was sexually molested as a child. Her mother passed away when she was 13 years of age, leaving her and her younger sister with a stepfather who was good to them but unable to give them what they needed. They moved in with different family members, going separate ways. She began working at an early age to pay for her piano lessons. She met the man of her dreams while attending Ahren's Night School and married shortly thereafter. They had three children and while they were still young, the love of her life was killed in a car accident, leaving her with the tasks of raising those children alone. She was scarred by an undesired divorce after remarriage. She had foot drop and experienced the trauma of breast cancer twice. She had a heart valve replacement and congestive heart failure, coming close to death and later receiving a diagnosis of Alzheimer's and dementia.

The introduction including some of her life's negatives is to show reasons, much like Job in the Bible, for her to have become a bitter person, taking that hostility to her grave. She chose faith, much like Job, which is accompanied by the first three letters of her name, **Joy**! The kind that came through her relationship with Jesus Christ. The only kind that allowed her to forgive the father who was not there for her and extend that same forgiveness to the woman who was responsible for killing her husband. The joy that shows up amid chaos and the joy that allows you to forge purpose from your pain. That same joy made her a servant caring for those she knew and loved but also for those she knew not of, up until her final breath. She was the mother who would give her children the benefit of any doubt yet inform them in the most counseling and apologetic way when they were wrong, the grandmother who would drive distances to prepare biscuits and gravy for her grandchildren or spend time with them at the drop of a hat, the friend who would always show up when needed, the person who would love and always include her extended family. She loved people, all people. She was adamant about that love when it came to Internationals leading her to China multiple times to teach English and I'm sure share her faith as boldly as she could amid Christianity restrictions. She bonded with people like no other. Even though she and her life were not perfect, the light seen here is the one that shines its brightness in a clouded and dark world that could have been her demise.

Lord, I pray that Thy Word – all of
may become personalized in
my life – In Jesus Name,
JH

The Light

Isaiah 9:2 (NIV) - "The people walking in the darkness have seen a great light; on those living in the land of deep darkness a light has dawned."

Psalm 27:1 (NIV) - "The Lord is my light and my salvation – whom shall I fear? The Lord is the stronghold of my life – of whom shall I be afraid?"

John 9:5 (NIV) - "While I am in the world, I am the light of the world."

John 1:5 (NIV) - "The light shines in the darkness, and the darkness has not overcome it.

Matthew 5:13-14 (NIV) – "You are the salt of the earth...You are the light of the world. A town built on a hill cannot be hidden."

♪

Tenderness at Twenty-two

Her life 'til then brimming with tears, happiness evolved as well
She worked just as her mother did, but education, she didst dwell
She found a night school to enroll and then began her term
More than learning to entrust, a love would soon affirm
Her classmate had a brother, available no doubt
She didn't realize school would take another route
Upon that initial meeting, she did fall immensely hard
Her heart did stir quite suddenly forgetting what was scarred
Who knew education and love, together she'd pursue
She certainly found both at the age of twenty-two!

♫

Truelove

Her strength, where does it stem, through the years with so much grim?
At thirteen her mother died, her father's love would soon subside
Early years, things occurred, a child should never endure
Trusting those who seemed okay, resulting in a lure
She knew some who loved her, they often held her close
Embraced her to show love, must have been the proper dose
Did she feel abandoned, and unloved by the ones who left?
Was her heart in shambles, taken in thought by theft?
Was there balance between those who left and those who seemed to care?
It seemed as though there surely was by so much love she'd share
She always said when dad did pass, our father from above
Something learned and upheld, somewhere found true love

♥

Love

Please don't tire of our love story, it's like that of no other
You would surely understand if you've ever loved a mother
Many our childhood years, she served as both you see
A mother and a father to her party of three
Doing the best she could, seems we never missed a beat
Providing for our needs, looking back, a monstrous feat
If your loved one has passed or still present with you now
Ponder, visit, call on them, whatever thy heart will allow

On the Road to Damascus

It was the year of 2013 when my family and I began noticing changes in our mother. She had undergone major surgeries in 2011 and 2013 and at the beginning I felt it may have been confusion aroused by the anesthesia. She became somewhat violent in the recovery room, pulling out the IV administered to her. It was odd enough to cause concern knowing it was unusual since she had undergone surgeries before. We soon realized with the confusion, questions, grief, and many uncharted characteristics, it did not come from this origin. Many questions have and continue to flood my brain concerning how we arrived to this point. Our world became different than how we had known it to be for so long. The truth is, it became just another detour in our journey of life and no different than any other calamity that strikes the lives of all of us on this planet.

There were multiple signs my family and I recognized at one point or another. Mom had the occasional forgetfulness, the kind many of us have from time to time, whether it is forgetting a name or a well-known restaurant but remembering its food. She was having trouble with the credit and debit entries in her checkbook and eventually began to forget to take her medicine. We would observe dents in her car and her side mirror being broken without the memory of how it became that way. There were conversation hints as well. But one day, it was to be just another day working at the voting polls for her, which she always loved doing. Meeting new people and getting paid to do so was a bonus for sure! Her call to inform me of her arrival came much later than expected. I asked what happened and her reply was that she just could not find the location, as if someone had picked it up and placed it somewhere else. You see, what should have been a ten-minute drive from home ended up being a two hour long journey requiring her to stop at a local convenience store to ask for directions to a location she had been numerous times. This sign was the one having the greatest impact for me in pointing us in a direction many of us fear for a loved one or even ourselves. As I thought about what had happened, my thoughts drifted to what if she had encountered the wrong person while asking for directions? What if she had hit someone or something while driving? I thought about how dreadfully frightened she had to be, like a young child amid ongoing traffic unable to recognize her whereabouts and just needing to feel some form of safety.

Mom always had a silliness about her, a naivety if you will. She would be the only person laughing after dinner while doing dishes finally getting the joke told at the table.

This was different....

"Wow, What is God going to do in our circumstances." JM.

♪

Signs

A heart valve had to be replaced, wasn't working as it should.
We were worried and concerned but knew with God, it would.
While in recovery, lost her mind, agitation did set in,
At one point they shocked her thrice, her skin was white and thin.
The next step was rehabilitation, encouraged as we were,
It was not the best experience, some trouble had to stir.
It was this time we began to see confusion take its course,
Difficulty to say the least to find the major source.
I still say unto this day, it is where it all began,
The journey we are on today, from then and through its span.

*

A heart valve she did receive, we thought it went quite well,
Until some changes soon began and things seemed to take a spell
Was it the anesthesia, a UTI to bout?
Or was it something dormant waiting to get out?
Confusion was what I witnessed, a different type or sort,
Was it one to last indefinite or would it be cut short?
So much going on at once, it's difficult to assume,
One over the other, leaving too much to consume.

The Diseases

They resemble the verse found in the Bible, **John 10:10, "The thief comes only to steal, kill and destroy"** and although the journey reminds you every day of the first part of this verse, it is the second sentence that says, **"I have come that they may have life, and have it to the full,"** truly revealing the destination to another world. After a visit to my mother's general practitioner and a simple but horrifying in office test, we received a diagnosis of Alzheimer's in 2013. She stayed in her own home and we continued to care for her there. My older brother had been staying with her, giving me solace at night knowing he was there. I continued to make sure her medications were taken and food eaten throughout the day. There were many phone calls expressing her fear of knowing something was off but could not put a finger on what it was. I remember being at camp with my daughter Shiloh, and answering Mom's phone call, not only hearing but feeling the fear in her voice, leaving me feeling hopeless and fearful for her myself. It was not long after that initial diagnosis that we talked to a group of Geriatric doctors who eventually took over her medical care. The practice included a social worker, General Practitioner specializing in the diseases, Neurologist and Psychologist. It was during this time we received the probability of her also having Vascular Dementia resulting from her heart issues. We only went to the doctor a handful of times, seeing mostly the General Practitioner for follow ups, blood work, medication refills, etc. We never saw the Neurologist or other professionals in the office who were suggested to us. At the time, I felt I would approach things as needed. At one time, I requested an MRI to be done on her brain to possibly see the damage being done by the diseases, but because she had a pacemaker, they couldn't perform one.

Alzheimer's and dementia are predictable and unpredictable contradictory as it sounds. They are predictable in the sense that you know there will be definite memory loss and at times contribute to some terrible, horrible, no good, very bad days and nights. Because the diseases affect the brain and everyone is different, unpredictability comes to play via behavior and thinking processes. I have a cousin who in her 70's was diagnosed with dementia. In her case, she has no filter, will sporadically share untruths that her mind creates and believes, and while she may have bad days, she is most of the time gregarious. My uncle who is in his 90's still maintains memory but ventures to conversation that puts his past self in the present, like sharing his work in installing flooring at the Assisted Living he's living in now. As of now, both seem to know who we are when we visit.

The diseases can cause quite an array of changes and behaviors. Although the more I pondered on how they affected mom, I realized it was no different than anyone else having a difficult day or a pleasant one. I think as a caregiver, it was easy at times to look for things to occur and instead of recognizing she was having a bad day the assumption of it being a disease related effect gave room for a growing hatred for it. A side effect of our fallen world is allowing the negatives to outshine the positives, allowing a domination of such. There were many bad days for mom (us): behavioral issues, probably stemming from independence withdrawal, embarrassment, and confusion. There were also many great days. I would take her to an adult day center a few days a week while I worked. We referred to it as "her work". She even asked me if she got paid for her services (playing the piano or whatever she engaged in). I told her she did knowing in my mind her payment came in the form of exercising her cognitive abilities. One morning we pulled up to "work" and there was a woman obviously desiring to leave pacing in front of the doors with her eyes expressing her wish for the door to open allowing her to escape. I mentioned to mom that maybe she would be able to console her when she got inside.

Knowing mom couldn't remember who I was in the mornings, it was a verbal thought. Upon picking her up that afternoon, one of the women working expressed her appreciation for all mom had done that day. Mom surprisingly asked, "what did I do?" She told her how she brought comfort and consolation to the woman we saw that morning and how she was able to get her to sit and eat by telling her she was not going to eat until she did (something Shiloh took credit for using it on mom a time or two). Mom had loved her. My mother had bad days which made me hesitant to talk about the good knowing it could turn on at any given moment. That's how the negative energy of Satan wanted me to feel, wants you to feel. This experience served as a constant reminder to me as well as others that throughout the duration of your long sufferings and disappointments, God not only wants you but needs you and will use you to help others. We just need to have a willing heart even when our mind says otherwise; this is meant for the caregiver as well.

I hear people groan relentlessly about how cruel and devastating the diseases of Alzheimer's and dementia can be. While I know from experience the truth in those groans, amidst being a caregiver, the dwelling on that truth adds nothing to your sustainability. It's like any other adversary and preparation for battle, you **"Stand firm then, with the belt of truth buckled around your waist, with the breastplate of righteousness in place, and with your feet fitted with the readiness that comes from the gospel of peace. Take up the shield of faith, with which you can extinguish all the flaming arrows of the evil one. Take the helmet of salvation and the sword of the Spirit, which is the word of God." Ephesians 6:14-17 (NIV).**

I know it reads and sounds a lot easier than it is, but I really can't tell you how in the world we would have maneuvered through without the foundation of those verses. I'm not going to lie or attempt to fabricate: the whole care-giving venture is a challenge for the strongest of individuals. One of my biggest pet peeves is thievery, so to see a thief at work right before my eyes adds a whole new dimension. Little by little you witness the enemy trying to take everything away from your loved one, creating a domino effect to stealing from you. Every evening mom would hold her head as if she felt the scrambling of her brain as it drifted away from her trying to figure out what's going on. One morning she asked why Roxanne did not come to visit her. While I did not want to carry out that conversation, I walked her through it, telling her who I was, and it came to her that I was her baby girl.

Her memory was lost within seconds. We dealt with short term memory loss quickly igniting the repetition that would serve as ammunition of the enemy. The diseases eventually took their course with her long-term memory as well. While her memory of who we were would come and go, we embraced the times she knew who we were and went along during the times she didn't. My advice to you is to embrace the innate creativity and find new in your loved one and know that no matter how they are affected, their souls still exist creating a sense of purpose and stability if even for a moment.

♪

We went to camp one year, a time we'd ne'er forget
My little girl and I, it didn't seem a threat
I'd talk to mom on the phone to check to see her day
She'd be so confused, with fear to our dismay
I'd try to calm her with my words, to put her mind at ease
It'd sometimes work tho' sometimes not, asking, "God, please?"
Surrounded by believers soon helped my troubled soul
Praying and believing, once again my soul was whole

♫

Stages

They tell me there are stages, I try at best not to dwell
My anxiety and stress levels will begin to swell
The disease goes back and forth not easy to conclude
Days and nights are different with any given mood
I'm finding it much easier to take each day by day
Ignoring those given stages, in the moment I will stay
The future I wish not to look, contemplating her demise
It's easier to tend to her and look into her eyes
Where oh where is your sting though death may come about
While we're on our journey no reason for to doubt

♯

Diseases

It's truly scary, the diseases, is what they all say
so much information to address and try to weigh
Everyone is different and effects just the same
Sometimes you have to play by ear, making it a game
One true thing shared by all is memory loss no doubt
Wondering how in the world everything gets out
The world in which they live certainly is beside
the one we're all in together, the one we all reside
We know there's another world waiting for us all
May we live to see it by answering our call

♪

Thief

I've never known a thief as unconscionable as it
Taking little by little to see what it can get
The piano she played, just as recently you see
She looks for me to play, she can't seem to find the key
The last of hope held on to, a release for her as well
We've got to keep moving forward, this mountain we won't dwell
Where's your sting Alzheimer's thief, trying to kill our joy
The officer in Jesus wipes away your evil ploy

♫

Further Along

It's taking a different turn now, at times she cannot see
Her hearing seems to be affected, looking at other than me
Little things we take for granted are those with no control
It has to be frustrating, gradually taking its toll
Giving her few options has finally run its course
Her mind cannot decide, I'll choose from whence the source
To focus on the task at hand when trying to partake
Her fork will drop or maybe food, her hand doth surely shake

Independence

Early on, I would witness the independence of mom disintegrate casting fear and doubt. She would share that she felt like she was no longer in control. But are we ever truly in control? That's a question given to her knowing she knew Who was in control and one that would be repeated multiple times. Independence is impossible. We go through life expressing the desire to become independent. Our flesh desires praise and a need to prove itself but from the moment we are born into this world we have a dependence. We depended on our mother to care for their bodies while carrying us. We depended on our parents to protect us and care for us through our younger years even into our early adult years. We become dependent on friends to pull us up when needed. We depend on the prayers of others, our relationships, and even the weather upon occasion. We depend on food to nourish us and water to hydrate us. When the diseases strike someone and what we have called our independence, we are taken by surprise by the lack thereof when it is gradually taken away. It is a difficult witness if we look at it through the eyes of the flesh. We see others, whether it be our parents, spouse, or other loved ones dwindle to a dependence we never saw coming. The truth is, it's something that has been rooted ever since Adam and Eve felt their need for independence was stronger than their dependence on God as we read in Genesis 3. Doesn't this all sound familiar?

My mother was born in 1933, experienced and survived way more than I could imagine. She attributed her survival to her dependency on God. After her diagnosis of AD/dementia, she had a challenging time grasping and accepting she was not in control of her life. She had many years of knowing Who was and always acknowledged it. The disease presented itself with a more challenging acceptance of that dependency. I get what she meant: just having that feeling of being able to make decisions and living by them; but like it is with many diseases or setbacks, there is only so much we can attempt to deter them. It is like the story of Jacob and his dislocated hip in Genesis. Jacob was self-sufficient and comfortable with that, but because we are human and cannot control everything like we would prefer, sometimes we need to realize where and to Whom our dependency lies. I have had many a hip dislocation in various forms and honestly caring for my mother was one, but one teaching me where my reliance should be.

Verses to help:

Psalms 62:5 (GNBUK) "I depend on God alone; I put my hope in Him."

Psalms 104:27 (GNBUK)- "All of them depend on you to give them food when they need it."

2 Corinthians 7:16 GNBUK)- "How happy I am that I can depend on you completely."

Psalms 62:1 (GNBUK) - "I wait patiently for God to save me; I depend on Him alone."

Romans 9:16 (GNBUK) - "So then, everything depends, not on what human beings want or do, but only on God's mercy."

Psalms 62:7 (GNBUK) - "My salvation and honour depend on God; He is my strong protector; He is my shelter."

2 Samuel 22:31 (GNBUK) - "This God – how perfect are His deeds, how dependable His words! He is like a shield for all who seek His protection.

Hebrews 12:2 (GNBUK) - "Let us keep our eyes fixed on Jesus, on whom our faith depends from beginning to end. He did not give up because of the cross! On the contrary because of the joy that was waiting for Him, He thought nothing of the disgrace of dying on the cross, and He is now seated at the right-hand side of God's throne."

1 Corinthians 2:5 (GNBUK) - "Your faith, then, does not rest on human wisdom but on God's power."

Matthew 5:3 (NIV) – Blessed are the poor in spirit, for theirs is the kingdom of heaven."

Thank You, Lord

Advocate

Being an advocate for your loved one should not begin when their earthly independence lessens. I have learned four ears and eyes are better than two and interpretations can always conflict or be learned from. I found myself always going with mom or taking her to her doctor's appointments. It is always a good idea to engage questions either of you may have and realize the questions thought of are not always the same. It also goes along with instructions given by a doctor for whatever specifics your visit entails. This pertains to hospital visits as well, where you have multiple staff turnovers and visiting nurses who may not know the history or medications of your loved one. Do not take for granted that they know just because they are present and healthcare workers. I remember once, a nurse's aide came in during a rehab visit to give her medication. She held it in her hand, and I asked her what the medication was but she did not know. I could not allow her to administer it to her until I learned what it was. It was later communicated to me it was illegal for her to be dispensing medication. That is a whole other story about facilities and their inability to keep knowledgeable and efficient staff present. There was also a time in the hospital when they did not have a ceased medication on file and was prepared to give it to her. It is so important to be that advocate for your loved one, to pay attention to details and the staff present treating them. Again, being a member in the healthcare profession does not mean they know everything they need to know about your loved one. We also experienced many other faults during rehab and hospital stays. I remember one stay, walking in seeing a puddle on the floor in mom's room causing it to be slick and no one to clean it up as quick as it should have been. In another facility for rehab and long after the diagnosis of the diseases, she had fallen breaking her wrist and fracturing her pelvis while under their care. She had also become very hostile, a side effect of Alzheimer's, commonly known as Sundowner's or a urinary tract infection. I informed their healthcare workers that she must have a UTI because of the differences between this and our experiences with the Sundowner effects. UTI's wreak havoc with the elderly and their brains. They tested multiple times at my request because the test result continued showing some presence of infection but they felt it was not enough to begin an antibiotic. I had even taken a picture of her urine upon getting a sample and it was completely swamp water, dark as can be. I knew my mother and what affected her more than they did. After finally getting her released from that facility and taking her to her general practitioner, we received a definitive presence of a UTI and given antibiotics, providing both of us some relief. In many cases at the rehab facility, I would also retrieve water or a necessity for mom and even a clean-up when needed. While we were blessed with many wonderful healthcare professionals, the reality is no one works on our timeline and well, the lack of staff in a hospital or rehab facility may dictate when something can be addressed by personnel. We are their true caregivers whether they reside with us or not.

One of the most important things you can do with your loved one preferably before they reach the need for a caregiver is to make sure they have a will including a document stating you or whomever it may be as their caregiver, listing a Power of Attorney and Health Advocate. Again, it is better to have it done while they still maintain some logic so they can contribute to those decisions. Eventually, they may forget because of the disease but it will assist you as their advocate to feel some ease knowing they had a hand in making that decision. You may still get hit with "you took my home away from me," or "you don't know what's best for me.," but you know when they were well, they felt their confidence in you enough to put you or whomever in that position. That is what you need to remember when the going gets tough. It is a difficult conversation, but one desperately needed. If you have children of your own, you could begin the conversation with your loved one or whomever you're caring for by stating the need to put something in place for your future. Even if no children are involved, you should still seek someone to appoint as your caregiver and/or health advocate. Thankfully, my mother and I had completed our wills and appointments together and while I did not remember at the time how it was originally stated, I am grateful to have had it. I was listed as Mom's Power of Attorney and first Health Advocate with my brothers listed as Health Advocates 2 & 3. While I could make the easy day-to-day decisions with both living out of town at the time, this allowed us to make crucial decisions together concerning issues that would arise later in our journey of Alzheimer's and dementia.

Thank You, Lord.

♪

Age should not decipher if they should go alone,
Whether they're a child or that of fully grown
It's like playing that story game whispering in one's ear,
Only to pass it on, various stories oh, to hear.
Their eyes and ears if need we be at some point in their life,
We need to help them navigate through any fear and strife.

♫

Multiple ears, it's always good with so much being told,
I would hear one thing as she would hear a load.
The medications they'd submit leery of their use,
Some research I would do at times giving an excuse.
To try and find another, no side effects to wear,
And one not to counteract with those already there.

♥

As I was growing up, an advocate she would be,
I never had to feel alone, she'd always be with me. When
I had to go to the doctor, no remembrance of fuss,
Having that heart of a mother was definitely a plus.
It didn't matter what I did, I knew that she'd be there,
Sadness, fear, overwhelming thoughts, alone not to bear.

Caregiver

"We cannot change the outcome, but we can affect the journey." -Ann Richardson-

Being an advocate is detrimental in any phase of life. Becoming a caregiver is a choice made when the time reveals evidence of the necessity for more assistance. To be clear let us decipher the difference in care giving and care taking. In my mind, if you say those words and focus on them, it's clear what your role would be. You would be giving care to your loved one, a more personal intimate approach, not taking it. Deciding to become a primary caregiver is truly a personal decision with many aspects to consider like logistics, POA, established health advocacy, availability, willingness with love, immediate family, etc.

In 2016, as the disease began to accelerate, a situation arose, and I knew we'd have to make a decision for mom's care. One day I went to check in on her and found her in a pool of blood in her bed not knowing at the time she'd had a bout of diverticulitis. Of course, having Alzheimer's, she didn't even realize it. It was that event that led me to know there would need to be a change. Honestly, I don't know why I felt the need to be her caregiver. It just felt like the natural thing to do. During the initial phases, I witnessed the presence of God and His perfect timing. As difficult as it was, I could sense God having set up my life to do what was needed to be done. Maybe it was one of those detours God enables to test my availability. I had my daughter who was 10 years of age and husband who mentioned it would be easier if we were all under the same roof and I knew it needed to be a family affair. I was retired from the Fire Service and worked part time at a school. I knew she couldn't join us where we were living at the time, so I looked urgently for a place more conducive, safe, and family friendly for all of us. I knew, at least in my heart there would be no one able to care for mom like I could, knowing her as I did and who she was her entire life. While my brothers lived out of town for many years, mom and I always resided in the same city. Maybe, I felt that sense of protection. Mom had always taken care of me, of us. Too, there is something to be said about a mother and daughter relationship as I'm finding out from the other side with my own. I embraced that and although my brothers would have done anything they needed to do for mom and did, the respect and dignity of day-to-day tasks as a caregiver needed to be embraced as well. While I always had a closeness with my mother, I'm sure we kept secrets from one another, but it was indeed a healthy relationship. We had our own separate lives engaging with one another as family members do. During our journey, I found scripture to validate our care-giving decision:

1 Timothy 5:4 (NIV) says, "But if a widow has children or grandchildren, these should learn first of all to put their religion into practice by caring for their own family and so repaying their parents and grandparents, for this is pleasing to God."

This was an opportunity to experience God's timing. Each leg of my own journey came with questions like, "Are you sure God?" "Are you sure it can't wait, or maybe look for something better?" Have you ever been faced with a task that made you question why and how on God's green earth you would ever get through it? So far, it has been the story of my life. I have been given challenges I did not realize until I was in the throes of situations, broken marriage, infidelity, self-doubt, non-traditional profession, etc.

At the age of 27, I was hired as one of the few females on the Louisville Fire Department. That in and of itself was challenging to say the least. The fact I knew what a fire truck was did not prepare me for the profession itself, let alone having to deal with those who were not accepting of me. At the age of almost 47 and 20 years on the department, experiencing God's sense of humor, I became a first-time mother gifted with a baby girl named Shiloh who didn't seem to come with instructions and who would become a prominent soul in a future that could have broken me. After being raised in the church my whole life, it was at this time, her conception and birth that would become my revelation. At a time when I thought I had everything I needed or wanted, trying to set the course of the future myself, I was reminded of **Proverbs 19:21 (NIV) - "Many are the plans in a person's heart, but it is the Lord's purpose that prevails."** and **Jeremiah 29:11 (NIV) - "For I know the plans I have for you, declares the Lord, plans to prosper you and not to harm you, plans to give you hope and a future."**

It was a revelation that would culminate into lessons of selflessness, honor and love, of which I apparently needed then and in my future. As I continue to navigate life with its ever-changing challenges and detours, and the surprise of each new one raising my level of anxiety a notch, I am reminded of God's promise of never leaving nor forsaking me, and that how you respond to what life throws at you impacts your life more than any other factor, something I learned in the beginning of life from my mother.

As I researched the topic of caregiving, many discrepancies existed between cultures. According to CEOWORLD magazine in 2020, our country, the United States, is not listed in the top 10 best countries in the world for the elderly to live in and yet, we are not listed in the top 10 of the worst countries in the world for them to live in. We, as a society in a country where nearly all states reference God or the Divine in their constitutions according to a 2017 Pew Research Analysis, accept and normalize that the responsibilities of taking care of our aged should fall on someone else. Many cultures grow up with an innate understanding that they will take care of aged family members with honor. According to a 2022 Colorado

State University article on Healthy Aging, "Eastern cultures treat older adults with more respect being guided by Confucian values that include a positive view of aging encouraging younger generations to treat their elders with respect, obedience and care." According to International Scholarly Research by Hindawi, "Caregiving was found as right and correct by all the focus groups. However, for some of the groups, caregiving was an expected part of life that was passed down from generation to generation." "Asian American, Hispanic American and African American participants reported seeing multiple examples of caregiving, not just within their own families but throughout their communities." I spoke recently with a couple, the husband from Vietnam and his wife from Venezuela. They both shared with me their mutual cultural bond of taking care of family. I was so impressed and validated when and after talking with them. They shared that nursing homes were extremely uncommon in their respective countries. Western Civilization puts more emphasis on their young and the busyness of life, sidelining the value of spending time with their elders let alone caring for them. I was so blinded by false assumptions and expectations before becoming a caregiver but during and even after my mother was gone, did I realize how much discrepancy there is and how we could learn from other cultures and put Godly values into practice.

I know there are circumstances beyond our control to disallow the direct care of a family member. I believe God intends for us to care however we can, enabling the best care and provision we can find. It may be your becoming a part-time caregiver or even finding them the best care possible and having you as an overseer. So many people find their hands tied when it comes to accepting becoming a caregiver for the lack of assistance from anyone. We as a nation could do so much better than what is being done to provide care for our aged and assisting the caregivers.

"A village without the elderly is like a well without water." -African Proverb-

After we found our home and moved Mom in shortly thereafter, a battle began. It is one of the most difficult memories during our journey. She knew something was going on with her but could not understand it. Aforementioned, a strong woman born in 1933, independent as we know it and surviving much by that time. Need I say more? There were times I would find her downstairs, unwilling to return upstairs to go to bed because she wanted to be in her own home, feeling as if everything had been taken away from her. Even sleeping in her own bed became a reality it was not her bed. She would also go looking for her shoes and/or coat intending on walking home. That is when Shiloh would step in where I had trouble. Mom found solace in her. God used Shiloh to bring peace to mom amidst a debilitating disease. She had her days with her as well and we found ourselves constantly reminding one another that it was the disease and not our mom and grandmother. I would eventually learn the need to put myself in my mother's shoes in some form or fashion to understand what she was experiencing at least in part with the array of confusion not knowing what her brain was going through. It did not always bring clarity or peace during challenging times but served as a buffer when my brain would go there. Mom also knew enough to share her love and knowledge about the impact living together could have on a family and a marriage. In fact, that subject came up numerous times while we resided with one another. I would constantly be reminded of it. Was it an excuse to try and be free from us? Maybe, a concerned one, one I knew she was adamant about but something I did not want her to worry about. I knew she had concern in her heart, and I appreciated that. I felt that making the decision as a family would stand the test of time. Our family unit did not survive the journey with mom but I know beyond any doubt, it was not because of her or our decision to care for her. Our journey was complicated and sidelined by something I could not control. Being in the middle of caregiving and a toxic relationship leading to divorce at the same time ignited a dependence on God even more. It was a call for a wonderful counselor who taught me about boundaries enabling me to continue the tasks at hand of continued care for my daughter and mother. I'm also thankful for a prior mutual agreement for mom's care even though our commitments were not compatible. I would just advise you before you make the decision of becoming a caregiver in whatever capacity you choose to include your family, making sure everyone is on board. No, it doesn't mean everything will be easier or will persevere, but your heart will be covered during and later on if things go south. There will also be many other things to consider like Memory Care units, skilled nursing facilities and those who genuinely care about their residents enough to remind them to perform the simplest of necessities like going to the bathroom, eating, taking medications, and instilling purpose, etc. One thing that was difficult for me was acknowledging the need for respite. I would scope out times for mom and me to do something together giving Shiloh and her dad time alone and a break from the repetition or whatever behavior may have made itself known. I did plan short family vacations outside of Mom and it worked out. At times it was emotionally hard for me to try to arrange care giving for respite. My brothers were available many times when I would ask but even then, I would worry about her. That is when I had to truly give it up to the Lord, knowing it was all going to be okay. Do not second-guess yourself on your abilities. There will be days you will wonder where God is and then you will realize that He equips you with everything you need no matter what decision is made during your journey. The most important thing you can do with your decision making is to pray about it, asking God to give you discernment about whatever it is you are called to do.

> *"Suffering is only intolerable when nobody cares.*
> *One continually sees that faith in God and His*
> *care is made infinitely easier by faith in someone*
> *who has shown kindness and sympathy."*
>
> *-Cicely Saunders-*

Verses to help you:

Psalm 32:8 (NIV) - "I will instruct you and teach you in the way you should go; I will counsel you with my loving eye on you."

Ephesians 5:15 (NIV) - "Be very careful, then, how you live— not as unwise but as wise, making the most of every opportunity, because the days are evil. Therefore, do not be foolish but understand what the Lord's will is."

1 John 2:17 (NIV) - "The world and its desires pass away, but whoever does the will of God lives forever."

Psalm 55: 1 (NIV) - "Listen to my prayer, O God, do not ignore my plea."

Hebrews 10:36 (NIV) - "You need to persevere so that when you have done the will of God, you will receive what he has promised."

Psalms 46:5 (NIV) - "God is within her, she will not fall; God will help her at break of day."

Psalms 9:18 (NIV) - "But God will never forget the needy; the hope of the afflicted will never perish."

Mark 9:24 (NIV) - "I do believe; help me overcome my unbelief!"

1 Thessalonians 5:16-18 (NIV) - "Rejoice always, pray continually, give thanks in all circumstances; for this is God's will for you in Christ Jesus."

1 Peter 3:17 (NIV) - "For it is better, if it is God's will, to suffer for doing good than for doing evil."

Philippians 4:6 (NIV) - "Do not be anxious about anything, but in every situation, by prayer and petition, with thanksgiving, present your requests to God."

Joshua 1:9 (NIV) - "Have I not commanded you? Be strong and courageous. Do not be afraid; do not be discouraged, for the Lord your God will be with you wherever you go."

James 1:5 (NIV) - "If any of you lacks wisdom, you should ask God, who gives generously to all without finding fault, and it will be given to you."

2 Timothy 3:17 (NIV) - "so that the servant of God may be thoroughly equipped for every good work"

Proverbs 3:5 (NIV) - "Trust in the Lord with all your heart and lean not on your own understanding" (One of Mom's favorite verses)

Matthew 6:34 (NIV) – Therefore do not worry about tomorrow, for tomorrow will worry about itself. Each day has enough trouble of its own."

Psalm 121:1-2 (NIV) - "I lift my eyes to the mountains – where does my help come from? My help comes from the Lord, the Maker of heaven and earth."

Matthew 11:28 (NIV) - "Come to me, all you who are weary and burdened, and I will give you rest."

2 Corinthians 1:3-4 (NIV) - "Praise be to the God and Father of our Lord Jesus Christ, the Father of compassion and the God of all comfort, who comforts us in all our troubles, so that we can comfort those in any trouble with the comfort we ourselves receive from God."

Psalm 71:9 (NIV) - "Do not cast me away when I am old; do not forsake me when my strength is gone."

Zephaniah 3:17 (NIV) - "The Lord your God is with you, the mighty warrior who saves."

♪

She does not know why she is here; she feels she should be at home
It's got to feel quite devastating, unsafe, not idle, to roam.
Her mind makes me a culprit, someone who planned her way,
Making my mind unsure, should she leave, or should she stay?
I remember someone once told me, for her I know what's best,
I have to trust the love process and simply ignore the rest.
You have to do what you know is right, sacrifice to God's delight,
To persevere when your love is tried, builds within an eternal pride.

♫

Remember when you coddled me and loved me through the days?
You always seemed to work through each and every phase.
The things I am doing now, there's no way to repay,
I know it may sound quite honestly like that of a cliche'.
If I could just make you understand God's calling on my life,
Includes taking care of you when you are dealt with so much strife.
Difficult to fathom being my mother, my child,
the circle of life indeed, not to be reviled.

♥

Not Giving Up

It's difficult to give up on others when they never gave up on you,
Perseverance at its finest, a lesson through and through
Opportunities here and there, given times to say, "Enough"!
Quiet strength and love pursued, a love, 'twas quite tough.
Didn't matter what was played out, the infractions large or small,
"So long", "good-bye", "I'm done", never said, do I recall.
Some in life gave reason, to learn to say good-bye,
Those who left voluntarily and those who would simply die.
To give up, a discernment of her heart and mind,
A natural sympathy, indeed, was not resigned.
A love like that, unnatural, exempt from all mankind,
Except to learn its origin, Christ's love is so defined.

Memory Loss

"I forgot where I laid my keys!" "I've misplaced my phone!" "I need my glasses to find my glasses!" "Inside my head, I'm hoping they introduce themselves to my friend because I cannot remember her name." "What was the name of that song?" "Who was the actor in that movie?" Sound familiar? Believe me, I have said all the above. It is a scary thought having already been through Alzheimer's and dementia with mom, making me wonder if I am headed in that direction. I know slow cognitive decline is expected as we get older, leading many of us to frustration and fear. Research continues to look for the causes of the diseases but from our experience I believe there may be many contributing factors including environmental, medications, anesthesia, etc. I've also read simple memory loss could be the result of health issues that if taken care of could be reversed. When dealing with memory loss due to Alzheimer's and dementia, there is a delivery of repetition. There is nothing like it and it is one of the most common frustrating challenges of being a Caregiver.

There may be situations that arise where you find yourself wondering if you need to remind your loved one of something they may have forgotten or even yet, did not know. For instance, when someone would come to my mother's mind, she would ask if they were still alive, I found myself telling her the truth if they had passed away and she would always ask, "Was I there?" It was so important for her to know that she was at the funeral. At the same time, I did not desire to multiply her grief. I had to take each situation at a time and deal with it as I felt led. I would be sure and take her to funeral visitations of anyone she was close to. It was important to her. As the disease progressed and some of her friends would pass away, I struggled with even telling her at all and at times, did not. In the beginning, short term memory loss was clear and evident. She could remember days gone by but had difficulty with what she had for breakfast or what happened the day before.

There were those days Shiloh and I were members of the family she grew up around. Many people deal with being forgotten by their loved one or thought of as someone else as with us. We just simply had to learn to go along with it, to engage in whoever she thought we were at any given moment. It kept us on our toes. I do know beyond any doubt and am grateful to feel she knew who we were upon taking her last breath.

Becoming accustomed to or tolerating repetition from memory loss is indeed challenging. I cannot stress that enough. Becoming accustomed to or tolerating repetition from memory loss is indeed challenging. Alright, enough already! Just getting you prepared if you are not already experiencing it. I know this subject may be short and will not compare to the long days full of repetition and I could include every day of our eight years, but that would take writing a book with sequels. After Mom's diagnosis there would be many a road trip taking Shiloh to gymnastics competitions, softball games, or even visits to see friends and family members. She'd already had a desire to read every billboard we would pass when she was not driving but take that multiplied by two, and if we traveled the same roads multiple times, we would know each season's billboard content for whatever city we were traveling to. For some reason, being in a vehicle seemed to compound the repetition and at times I felt we were in quite the tuna can. In the mornings as I was preparing breakfast, if she did not ask me once where "Betsy" aka Shiloh was, she would ask me a thousand times it seemed. This is where I truly learned the hard way, trial and error, of how to communicate in a respectful way after of course many days filled with annoyance, repetition of my own and ignoring. We learned to wear shirts with no writing on them or turn them inside out because of the non-stop questioning and educated sense about her. I would often give her a chore to do of folding clothes. Any clothing with words usually ended up wrinkled by the time they were folded. Watching television was quite challenging at times as well when she would constantly ask what had happened after repeatedly telling her. While there was always frustrated repetition, we did not always let it get the upper hand. There were times Shiloh and I both took advantage of that repetition with having our backs tickled the way she did when we were growing up. Other times repetition came in handy was when she needed to be doing something and I would give her a basket of socks to fold only to unfold them later, giving her the same basket to continue the process or when she was brushing her teeth. I do not think she ever got hip to the sock folding but she did tire of it, and she did have most of her teeth when she passed! When you think about it, she would tire of repeatedly folding socks much like I would tire of her repetition. It is a mystery, isn't it?

"Oh, my goodness, if I have to say that one more time!", "I already told you that", "Remember, I told you." These are words used by all of us if we find ourselves being asked the same question after giving an answer. It becomes quite irritating, wears on you after a while and believe me, you are not the only one affected. Your loved one or whomever you encounter having the disease could feel at any given moment an intense sense of confusion, sadness, and unworthiness. A part of their self-worth comes into play during the communication aspect. Many already feel or know there is something going on or wrong with them and how we respond to them can either help or harm them. Telling them you have already told them something once or multiple times is not going to assist your cause. Their logic does not exist. I know, I am guilty. Again, I had to put myself in my mother's shoes attempting to understand how I would have felt given the response she had been given at any moment. With that comes guilt, conviction, and apologies but the result makes you better for it.

During our journey, I had read and heard through a support group about the therapeutic lie. I do not think any of us were raised to lie to our parents or someone in authority. In fact, just the opposite and it was truly clear to me that I was going to have a tough time facilitating this form of therapy. I just continued to repeat myself and answer the call until I finally realized that respectfully ignoring after a given question and following it up with a different subject would at least allow some form of respite during that specific moment. At other times, in those precious morning hours, when I would be Auntie" and Shiloh, "Betsy," I would need to call our cousin RB, the son and brother of those two or text his daughter Sherri to ask questions I truly had no answer for concerning family members. I ended gaining an education at times. Could I have made something up? I could have if my brain of ill quick wit would have turned a leaf and I felt comfortable lying or gave birth to creativity any given moment but I just could not find the ability to do it. I did find myself fabricating a time or two in the heat of the moment asking under my breath for forgiveness. The realization during these moments was the reiteration of the phrase, "once a man, twice a child" and it's occurrence more than once during our journey. How many times for those of us with children in our lives did we have to repeat answers to questions multiple times feeling the same frustration? You may have to deal with it the way I did, through trial and error, calling loved ones for answers or you could be blessed like my cousin Scott and my uncle Tim with a gift of quick wit, dry or not, to be able to answer any given question without any monotonousness. I can tell you there were many informal conversations between God and I in the midst of many a morning that would push me through to the next part of the day.

Verses to help you:

James 1:19 (NIV) – My dear brothers and sisters, take note of this: Everyone should be quick to listen, slow to speak and slow to become angry."

Proverbs 15:28 (NIV) – The heart of the righteous weighs its answers, but the mouth of the wicked gushes evil."

Proverbs 12:25 (NIV) - "Anxiety weighs down the heart, but a kind word cheers it up."

Proverbs 15:1 (NIV) - "A gentle answer turns away wrath, but a harsh word stirs up anger."

Proverbs 18:21 (NIV) – The tongue has the power of life and death, and those who love it will eat its fruit."

Psalm 19:14 (NIV) – May these words of my mouth and this meditation of my heart be pleasing in your sight, Lord, my Rock and my Redeemer."

Repetition

Do you remember your own child or that of someone else?
The many times you had to speak, those repetition spells?
Unnerving about it all, it would take you through the roof,
Until you had to stop and think, realizing she's aloof.
Alzheimer's and dementia attack in many a unique way,
They know just what to do to over-extend their stay.
Frustration for the caregiver is common you must know,
Keep in mind the love you have, how God will help you grow.

♪

Ten times in a three-minute span surely runs its course,
I ask myself, "how many times can I repeat this source"?
After some time, some years, it begins to be the norm,
Somehow you feel within yourself to battle through the storm.
The mind with its intricate parts way beyond my grasp,
If I could only understand, my thoughts are such of rasp.

♪

She asks me every morning, "Is Betsy already up?"
I tell her for the hundredth time and say "Lord, take this cup"!
She's always had concern straight from discerning heart,
Why not comprehend, in her mind, she plays a part.
There are ways to get around it, trial and error at its best,
Ignore her, change the answer, put her to the test.
All things, always temporary, believe it to be true,
Don't look back at conclusions you wish you hadn't drew.

♫

Remember the toddler you experienced, someone else's or your own?
All the non-stop questioning made you wish that they were grown.
It's going to be turned up a notch because indeed they are,
You think that then was hard, now it's going to seem bizarre.
It begins with just a question, maybe once, for they forgot,
As disease progresses, it changes to a different plot.
Repeating is monotonous, ignoring might come next,
Talking to yourself can surely make you feel perplexed.
Take a break, walk out, return when you feel at ease,
You can always say "I'm sorry, forgive me if you please".

♪

She Calls Me Auntie

She calls me "Auntie" in the mornings, I can't be upset with that,
One of my favorite people who for me, she'd go to bat.
Auntie took her in as if she were her own,
One of the selfless people I have ever known.
She raised and loved her, a peace she would embrace,
Never did she feel alone or that of a displace.
So, whenever she's confused, I have learned to flow along,
So much like that of Auntie, she needs to feel where we belong.

♫

She Calls Her Betsy

She calls her granddaughter "Betsy", Auntie's daughter she would be,
I think she knows the difference but her memory dost she see.
The day will linger on, Betsy's in and then she's out,
Then Shiloh will appear and you'll know without a doubt.
When she was but a child, mom cared for her at best,
The love between the grands is certainly one blessed!

♥

The Love Between the Grands

I don't know what it is or if as a parent I'll ever learn,
The love between the grands, something to discern.
At times the difficulty of caring for her needs,
is in fact a battle with discouragement and pleads.
It often has me shaken, feeling to walk away and pause,
I think, what in the world could assist me with this cause?
Then turning to the familiar face would certainly show love,
The peace found came through Shiloh, fitting as a glove.

Dignity

One of the most valuable God given gifts that all of us have is our dignity. One of the easiest things to rob someone of is their dignity and the more I am surrounded by older folks I realize they're not only vulnerable to being taken advantage of but there is such an opportunity to witness dispossession of that dignity. I believe existing in the world we live in makes us all vulnerable to doubting that gift God gives us and the ones who rob us of it knowingly or not. The ones with Alzheimer's and dementia are challenged from the beginning when they sense the changes within them, having to depend on others up until the end of life. My mother was a very modest person who would always tell me that "pretty is as pretty does." It did not mean she didn't enjoy dressing up, make-up, fixing her hair, etc. For me, I had no problem assisting her with personal tasks regarding hygiene, but to the one on the receiving end, it can become a dignity thief. As a caregiver, it is important to concentrate on building your loved one up and making sure others do the same, making them feel worthy and honored. It becomes challenging because you yourself become exhausted, but if God exhausted His efforts with us, we would be in big trouble. I found myself praying for patience constantly until someone shared not to pray for patience because just like exercise, you must grow into it and growing means testing, ha! It was better to go with the flow and live as if I had been helping mom her whole life.

Your loved one may feel they can still clean themselves after using the bathroom not realizing they really cannot, without a mess. I remember finding it helpful to say things like "I know it's difficult to reach all the way back there, so I'm happy to help", "Let's just double check to ward off a UTI." At times I would remind her of all the times she cleaned me growing up. Of course, it was many times counteracted with, "well, you're my baby girl." When the need for adult briefs have become a reality, there are ones that look like actual underwear with light to heavy coverage that may help with the transition.

When it came to shower time, I would allow mom to shower herself monitoring her outside the curtain. I installed a handrail inside the shower wall giving her more support while maneuvering. After a while, I eventually purchased a shower chair and would help her sit down, allowing her to wash herself and then use her walker seat as support once she stepped out. The shower chair also came in handy when she fractured her pelvis. It took a little more to pick her up to get in and out but we got it done. In the latter stage of the disease when she could not walk, I would use the foam no rinse cleanser and then lotion her up. I truly received the blessing being able to do these things for mom. I knew she would feel better being taken care of in that way on account of not being able to do it completely herself. I also knew our time was limited and while the disease would steal much, during moments of clarity, I was reminded of her servant's heart. When it came time for the routine after bathing, I tried to implement everything she would while getting ready: her deodorant, body lotion, make-up, hair, and teeth. Again, initially she could still perform everything herself until she couldn't. At that time, I would find myself becoming a hair-dresser by trimming her hair, a make-up artist, and personal stylist keeping her style intact. Another must included her lipstick which she never went anywhere without. Having to do what you never thought you would will eventually become natural to you. I know many who find it difficult with a parent of the opposite sex but I believe God will put you in professional mode to allow you to complete the tasks at hand. At times you run on impulse and adrenaline. Did I always get it right? No! Did I forget or was I lazy to put her lipstick on? Yes!

Attempting to emulate your loved one's actions toward their own self-care before they couldn't should always be a welcomed gesture. Offer them a Spa-day or even take them to have their nails done. Always remind them Who they belong to and how worthy they are.

Verses to help you:

Job 40:10 (NIV) – "Then adorn yourself with glory and splendor, and clothe yourself in honor and majesty."

Titus 2:7 (NET) - "showing yourself to be an example of good works in every way. In your teaching show integrity, dignity, and a sound message that cannot be criticized…"

1 Corinthians 10:31 (NIV) - "So whether you eat or drink, or whatever you do, do it all for God's glory."

Philippians 2:13-14 (NIV) "for it is God who works in you to will and to act in order to fulfill his good purpose. Do everything without grumbling or arguing.

Proverbs 31:25 (NIV) - "She is clothed with strength and dignity; she can laugh at the days to come."

"Every life deserves a certain amount of dignity, no matter how poor or damaged the shell that carries it." - Rick Bragg-

♪

Don't forget their dignity, they need to feel their worth
Fix their hair and make-up or what will grant them mirth.
What is it to bring a smile to someone who's lost their way,
It has a lot with what you do and not just what you say.
Her hair and her lipstick, both necessities to say the least,
making her feel beautiful as her ability has decreased.
Is it extra work, do you think you're doing enough?
A few more minutes to see that smile can't be all that tough.

♫

Never a day would go by without her looking glam,
Even as she aged and she became a gram.
Although her mind would tell her, "You're not beautiful at all",
Her heart became the reason she could stand above it tall.
She always told me, "Pretty is as pretty does", evident to see,
She of course, just didn't talk, she walked it just for me.

♪

Visualizing beauty is not just for the eyes,
It's knowing you have confidence and asking to be wise.
It's putting trust in someone, not relying on your own,
Displaying evidence of seeds selflessly sown.
If there were ever a question of God to be so real,
I look in your direction and see what you reveal.
In the midst of darkness, with all the chaos and unknown,
Your spirit still existing to let me know I'm not alone.

Purpose

If there's one thing that stands out in life with my mother, it's purpose! It's something that trickled down from her and what she taught without giving a formal class. She taught it through the life she led. All of us are born into this world to serve a purpose. **Ephesians 2:10 (NIV) says, "For we are God's handiwork, created in Christ Jesus to do good works, which God prepared in advance for us to do."** Sometimes we may not realize what that purpose is until it smacks us right in the face. I don't believe God intended us to retire our purpose as long as we're still existing on this planet. When our loved ones face the diagnosis of Alzheimer's and dementia and their cognitive skills are put to the test, many fear their lives are over, even the caregivers. Although it is a terminal illness, it presents us with an opportunity to take whatever time is left to live life to its fullest. Once that diagnosis is made, like mom, patients can immediately step into a depression knowing something is going on with them unable to pinpoint what. All she wanted to do was sleep and wake up with her reality just being a nightmare. While we know death is inevitable, embracing the reality of the beginning to your end can create a fear that can and will steal whatever joy that exist within. That's why we as caregivers and families of those affected should do everything possible to emphasize our loved one's purpose, finding ways to help validate their worth and the need for their existence. In other words, we need to nurture them, which may at times feel like an uphill battle when you wonder if it is doing any good or you dwell on the outcome of the disease. What does not feel like that at times when we, as a society, want immediate results? I would need to reiterate mom's counsel back to her in that as long as she had breath, she could serve. At home, I would give Mom chores to do even when she had succumbed to a wheelchair. I even utilized her and her wheelchair using them as an anchor on one end of the rug I was vacuuming. She would also fold clothes/socks as previously mentioned, wash windows which was something she loved doing and me, not so much. In the beginning, I would also have her help in the kitchen, paring vegetables or sorting them out. It was also extremely helpful when Shiloh would take her into her room and hang out making her feel loved and needed. Let your creative sense guide you or reach out to google to find ways to mirror something they may have previously enjoyed or been involved in before the disease. I once watched a video about a man who had Alzheimer's. He had been an engineer by profession and his daughter being his primary caregiver needed to find something for him to do. She came up with the idea of telling him a story about a company who would pay someone to pop bubble wrap. At first, he would be paid $5.00 for each sheet he popped until he had a moment of clarity and realized he should be being paid more. His daughter got him a $5.00 raise, ha! In the moment, it is difficult at times to think of things but honestly you do not need to look too deep into it. It is the simplest of things that could have an impact on allowing them to feel their lives still have purpose. We made sure the outdoors were a part of our day including the three of us hopping on the 4-wheeler and going for a ride, tossing the ball back & forth, implementing mom in my workout, taking her to the park to feed the ducks or back to the garden. We would many a morning eat our breakfast outside on the deck which is something she always enjoyed. She would accompany us pretty much everywhere we'd go, whether it was Shiloh's specific sport games, her school functions, church, Bible study, family/friend visits and of course the day centers she would attend. At times I had to emphasize the importance of her presence, like "Shiloh needs you there, she loves your cheering for her", "You're their only pianist, they need you.". Usually if it had anything to do with Shiloh, seeing her family members or church, it did not really take many words of encouragement for her willingness to go. There were times she just was not feeling well and desired to stay and rest but those were times I had to decipher whether she was physically ill or falling back into a depression. It is at times difficult to read them especially when they reach a point of not being able to communicate what they feel or if what they are feeling is valid since they could be telling you one thing and in reality experiencing something else. At some point, they may feel socially awkward at times fearing others responses to their illness but that's when we have to step up our game and reiterate their purpose in life and that God is not through with them yet. It can be a disconcerting task especially for those who dwell on their demise or if what we say to them, they comprehend. Whether our loved ones live with us or not, the important task of reminding them of their purpose can arise during any conversation and it should. Honestly, it is a relational topic that many of us need to be intentional about with ourselves and others. Encouragement is key and does not need to cease when someone has a terminal illness or a disinterested response. Love is the key. They'll feel it if only for a moment.

"You matter because you are you, and you matter to the end of your life. We will do all we can not only to help you die peacefully, but also to live until you die." -Cecily Saunders-

Verses to help:

Psalms 139:14 (NIV) - "I praise you because I am fearfully and wonderfully made; your works are wonderful, I know that full well."

Psalm 92:14 (NIV) - "They will still bear fruit in old age;

Romans 12:6 (NIV) - "We have different gifts, according to the grace given to each of us."

Jeremiah 29:11 (NIV) - "For I know the plans I have for you, declares the Lord, plans to prosper you and not to harm you, plans to give you a hope and a future."

Proverbs 19:21 (NIV) - "Many are the plans in a person's heart, but it is the Lord's purpose that prevails."

1 Corinthians 10:31 (NIV) - "So whether you eat or drink or whatever you do, do it all for the glory of God."

Jeremiah 1:5 (NIV) - "Before I formed you in the womb I knew you, before you were born I set you apart; I appointed you as a prophet to the nations."

Ecclesiastes 3:1 (NIV) - "There is a time for everything, and a season for every activity under the heavens."

Medications

Mom was not on a vast quantity of medications: thyroid, heart and cholesterol. To hear her tell it, she was a walking medicine cabinet. I always tried to downplay her medications by telling her about the patients we would make runs on while in the Fire Service and how we would carry out bags of medications for one patient. In the beginning of her diagnosis, we purchased a daily medication container including AM and PM slots to make it easier for her. As the disease progressed and she appeared to be forgetting to take her meds, a family friend offered us a battery-operated container where it would revolve with an alarm to the desired day and time which came in quite handy, even while we were living together. What a blessing it was!

When there's the diagnosis of the diseases and certainly signs and symptoms, the reality of accepting it as a terminal illness is difficult but one that should be embraced to assist the loved one and the caregiver. In many instances, probably more than not, many people get complacent with the medications they take and no offense, but doctors are no exception. If you don't address something concerning your medications or that of your loved one, the old adage, "if it ain't broke, don't fix it", will prevail.

With the diagnosis of Alzheimer's and/or dementia and two of their common traits being confusion and memory loss, it was important to research the medication taken as far as side effects and how they can conflict with the disease or with other medications. The doctors and drug manufacturers may say there are small percentages of counteractions and personally that's something you need to weigh out and figure through trial and error. The Alzheimer drug prescribed to mom was Namenda. After I researched and understood the side effects and possible counteractions, we kept her on it. It wasn't a cure but we were told it was to treat the symptoms. According to the Alzheimer's Association website, it's listed as a glutamate regulator and supposedly regulates glutamate which is a chemical messenger that helps the brain process information. We also attempted Donepezil (Aricept) along with the Namenda but mom didn't fare well with the Aricept and honestly with both medications sharing the side effects that corresponded with the behaviors of the diseases, she was taken off the Aricept but continued with the Namenda. I did ask for something that would assist in calming mom when there was anxiety or depression setting in. So, she was prescribed Sertraline (Zoloft) and given in small doses, once in the morning and once in the evening. It did not completely erase difficult times, but it seemed to assist some. That lasted until she was further along in the disease, and I questioned the need for continuance and she was taken off them. It is incredibly difficult to tell whether the medications are contributing to the quality of life when the effects of the disease begin to surmount. That is the question that always came to mind. Is the medication contributing to the continuance of the quality of life during mid to final stages of the disease or at all? In our experience with the diseases and their involvement of shrinking the brain with or without the use of medications, I will always wonder. I know of others using the same drugs I listed and seemed to do fair, as well as you can expect having the disease. It is all still a mystery. There is also the knowledge of everybody being different resulting in varying side effects and benefits. Mom's cholesterol medicine was a statin drug. Upon researching it, I found it could cause mental fuzziness and confusion. Well, we surely did not need to compound those areas. After consulting her General Practitioner and asking if we could cease the drug, she was taken off it and we never experienced any issues as a result thereof. She was also on medication for her heart, blood pressure and atrial fibrillation and I asked if it was necessary for her to take the dosage she was prescribed and it was cut in half. There were never any repercussions from that. The only other decision we as a family had to make was concerning her pacemaker battery. It was stated in the Power of Attorney papers that had been drawn up that her health surrogates, my brothers and I, could make the appropriate decisions regarding her healthcare and her quality of life when she no longer could.

When the battery was getting low and she was in the middle to late stages of the disease, we went to talk to her cardiologist asking what would happen if we did not replace the battery. We knew she would have to go through another sedation as well. We were told her heart rate would decrease to the 30's leaving her not feeling to do much at all. There were decisions we as a family had to consider and make and we did not desire mom to have to endure the prolonged effects of Alzheimer's and dementia. There was never anything that resulted from a difficult decision and her heart rate never went below 59 and lasted for over a year. All that being said, it left me questioning the need for particulars being prescribed and administered at all. I am not suggesting it would be the same for everyone, but it is worth the effort to research medications, finding out if what you are on or your loved one is truly conducive to the quality of life without adding to an already confused terminal state of being. Mom was also on a blood thinner because of her A-Fib. There were times this complicated even a nosebleed. As much as I would ask her to not blow her nose so fiercely, it would end in disaster, taking us a couple of times to the ER with an uncontrollable nosebleed. She would forget. She did not realize it. The blood thinner was a nightmare as well when I found her at the beginning of it all in the pool of blood from her diverticulitis bout leading us straight to the ER once again.

For an AD/Dementia patient, becoming ill is challenging for everyone involved. It's difficult to determine if they're not feeling well unless of course they have a fever. They at times don't even realize they're ill which is one of the blessings of the disease, I guess. Because confusion, agitation and aggressive behaviors are traits of the diseases, it can be difficult to make a diagnosis by naming symptoms in this case because those traits are also symptoms of a urinary tract infection experienced by the elderly as I mentioned previously. I realize medications have their purpose. I don't believe they are always needed for a quality of life as I experienced with mom. Do your research. You owe it to your loved one and yourself. Some of the best medications are those not prescribed by a doctor and ones we don't often give to mind. They are love, music, a cheerful heart, exercise, purpose, time spent, dignity, attention, and above all else as with mom, a relationship with Jesus Christ.

Verses to help:

Philippians 4:6 (NIV) - "Do not be anxious about anything, but in every situation, by prayer and petition, with thanksgiving, present your requests to God."

Philippians 4:7 (NIV) - "And the peace of God, which transcends all understanding, will guard your hearts and your minds in Christ Jesus."

Matthew6:25 (NIV) - "Therefore I tell you, do not worry about your life, what you will eat or drink; or about your body, what you will wear. Is not life more than food, and the body more than clothes?"

Proverbs 16:24 (NIV) - "Gracious words are a honeycomb, sweet to the soul and healing to the bones."

Proverbs 17:22 (NIV) - "A cheerful heart is good medicine, but a crushed spirit dries up the bones."

Proverbs 4:20-22 (NIV) – My son, pay attention to what I say; turn your ear to my words. Do not let them out of your sight, keep them within your heart; for they are life to those who find them and health to one's whole body."

♪

Giving her meds in the morning and a small amount to eat
Then visiting in the mid of day seemingly quite beat
She hadn't really eaten, slept most throughout the day
Questioning if I should leave or rather should I stay?
I knew depression was setting in, I could feel it at its core
Was it then making an appearance, the beginning of our war?
It's easy to comply to the meds they want to give
But are they really helping her to make her want to live?
Trial and error took its course until we had to stop
The medicines they prescribed we simply had to crop

Fitness

The importance of fitness (physical, mental, and spiritual) should never be underestimated or put on the back burner when it comes to patients with Alzheimer's and dementia and those who become caregivers. Okay, so, it's important for everyone! It seems a bit strange to speak the words of physical fitness and my mother in the same text. You see, she never enjoyed exercising or physical fitness. She did bowl quite frequently in her younger years and we have pictures to show for that. I also once witnessed her little body pick up and move a concrete bird bath by herself. I remember playing on a church softball team with her when I was a teen and we would always laugh when she would hit the ball and finally make it to first base via the pitcher's mound. She had a curve to her run and even with her drop foot, it never slowed her down. As she aged, as wisdom sometimes makes itself known, she realized her need to exercise was one she needn't overlook. Thankful for the Silver Sneaker's Program, she enlisted herself to a local gym and began her regiment of treadmill walking and other instructed moves finding that her specialty was making new friends and I'm pretty sure that is what kept her going. As far as mental fitness, she actually went to college receiving her Bachelor's degree while in her fifties. That was a feat in and of itself, realizing our memories are not what they used to be by then. Once your loved one is diagnosed and as their caregiver, you will need to implement these necessities for their quality of life. After mom was diagnosed and me being a fitness junkie myself and repeatedly saying we were not going down without a fight, the fight was not just going to be with the disease, knowing exercising was not her favorite thing to do. I knew she did not like to sweat, something I never saw her do. I knew she was just one of those people who just flat out had better things to do, like play the piano or serve others. While I know you can fit everything in, people have their priorities. I will say though that she would always participate wherever others were involved. After we moved and having attended a local gym, I found they had the Silver Sneaker's program and I could see the classes being held while working out myself. I thought it would be something she would enjoy especially if she could use her vocal cords and facial muscles to engage others while exercising. It was fun watching her engaged and even joining her in the exercises. It was not too long after that because of some acquiring limitations the disease provided, we had to discontinue and exercise at home.

Many people overlook and underestimate the power in exercising, especially those who are either not a fan or those who discount the value after they reach a certain age. The truth is the smallest amount of movement is better than none. Once we decided to continue at home, we came up with several movements. For instance, being in a seated position having her extend her legs at the knee one at time simulating a leg extension in the gym. Another was giving her very small dumbbells or even a canned good and having her perform curls with them one arm at a time beginning with her arms extended, bending at the elbow and raising the weight up. The seated calve raise was a good one for her ankles, feet, and calves. While seated with her feet planted firmly on the ground, she would lift her heels up and down. We also could implement the exercises we learned at the gym, like using a ball and having her hold it in both hands out in front of her squeezing causing tension to work her upper body and doing the same for her lower body placing it between her legs and having her push them together. Another fun one we would employ was throwing a ball back and forth, one which Shiloh enjoyed doing with her as well as keeping a balloon in the air. These are exercises that are good for body and brain. The agilities are movements in multiple directions within a matter of seconds that exercise the brain as well, something I'm enjoying now as I age. When I began taking mom to Adult Day Centers, they would implement some type of movement with exercises for the attendees. Movement is something you truly want your loved one to do. Muscle loss and atrophy can and will emerge after a period of inactivity.

On occasion I would again need to reiterate her own words pertaining to breathing, moving, and serving. I truly hope she realized that all her encouragement and cheer-leading was coming back to her instead of my being a slave driver.

Let us allow our loved ones to rest a bit while I explain how especially important physical fitness is for everyone, even a caregiver. It is just as important as having your loved one participating in it. I began lifting weights and exercising in my early twenties. It became a lifestyle for me and one as I am aging appreciate wholeheartedly. It surely assisted me in my profession and although my body aches with osteoarthritis, the prescribed medicine is to keep moving and that is exactly what I strive to do. I knew I had to set the example for my family. I cannot stress enough how important it is for anyone as a caregiver. It can be as simple as a walk or exercises at home. Protect your bones. Protect your heart and lungs. Protect your brain. As a caregiver, you may need to move your loved one from point A to point B and being in the best shape possible will enable you to do just that and at least assist you in using other appliances to help them move, like straps, chairs, etc. Exercise not only strengthens your body but also provides a release from all the tasks at hand. You can go away for a bit mentally while becoming stronger physically and the best part about it is you are never too old for it to be productive. When there is no physical activity or decreased activity because you think you haven't the time or you are too old to start, please consider the negative effects on your health, like increased anxiety, greater chance of falls, loss of strength and bone mass, high blood pressure, and believe it or not, decreased mental capacity among many other effects. There's a true to life saying that tells us we must take care of ourselves to efficiently take care of others. As a Christian, I'm told my body is a temple of the Holy Spirit, who lives in me. We do not belong to ourselves but to God. Honestly, there should be no question to caring for our bodies in all ways to be the best we can be in order to be used for His glory. So, when your mind tells you, "You can't", or assists in reiterating your dislike of exercise or fitness, you take control in changing that mindset for you and your loved one. Remember, take baby steps, celebrate small milestones on the way to becoming a healthier, better version of you. There's always time to exercise. I ceased going to the gym during caring for mom because of time and convenience and I set up my own little in-home gym. What helped me was rising early before everyone else, to get it done. When I included mom in my workouts, I would tie a rope on her transport chair and around my waist, using it as what the fitness world refers to as a sled and would pull her a short distance. I had to stop before I got too close to the top of our steep driveway; with her momentum, she'd be flying! Yeah, that wouldn't have been good. She enjoyed it too, so much she would say "Yabba dabba doo" while moving!

The mental/brain exercises we did at home and when she would go to the day centers were word games, seek and finds, crafts, coloring and having her read until she no longer could. These provided mental strength and more time with it. Even if they can no longer read, you could have them look at pictures and tell their own story. Another is talking to them about their past. In my experience, in the beginning many have short term memory loss and remember days and years gone by. I enjoyed talking to mom about her past. While much of it put me on an emotional roller coaster, it surely served as an education about her life and her strength to get through it. There's one exercise and talent mom fortunately enjoyed and used in serving others. Those piano lessons I mentioned earlier that she paid for herself became a God given gift and one she took seriously by paying it forward in a way that would end up blessing multitudes. She became a church pianist assisting in many cantatas and musicals. If you were one who sang off key, you'd definitely learn the key or lip sync during the time of her direction. There were many years of family holidays or visits gathering around the piano and singing hymns and nursery rhymes with the children. Music is such a universal glue and the musicality is definitely a gift for many. Mom would not be able to remember what she had for breakfast or who I may have been in any given moment, but she was able to sit at the piano and play for much of her life with Alzheimer's and dementia. In fact, she continued to play at church until I realized it was becoming much more difficult for her when she would make mistakes as the disease progressed. Mind you, everyone makes mistakes but there was just something unsettling witnessing her frustration. I knew I would have to ask God for discernment as I did with her driving capabilities concerning her continuing to play versus the frustration you rarely saw when she had it all together. In our doubt and dismay, God always saves the day. We were able to take her gift to the day programs where she became their pianist. Her idea of going to a place she would sometimes describe as a babysitting facility for adults quickly became her "job". The residents and employees truly valued and loved hearing her play. It was soothing to many and they loved singing along. There are many individuals I would read about and view on social media who shared the diseases, would be amid cognitive impairment and would suddenly be awakened by music and dance, enabling them to live in a moment of clarity and happiness. I believe even if they didn't or don't play a musical instrument or aren't experienced in the Arts, their minds are capable of much, listening to music from days gone by, which is soothing to the soul.

Another mystery! Never underestimate the power of music. I know at some point during your journey, you're going to question if it is all worth it. Are you wasting your time having them perform these menial tasks questioning the outcome and service to your loved one? I mean it is a terminal illness if they have dementia or Alzheimer's and even if not, they are aged. Put yourself in their position. Think about the alternative. You know, the one where they just lie around doing absolutely nothing resulting in expedient brain deficiency and muscle atrophy, giving you or any other caregiver more strenuous work to perform. If you are not doing anything yourself, use it as an opportunity to engage in something with your loved one. Set aside time and schedule it in your daily routine. It will become easier as you continue, and you will appreciate it as the days go by. Last but certainly not least is another area of fitness and that is of the Spiritual. I know without the faith passed down from my mother, my own revelation, and God's continued presence in both our lives, this journey would have been more challenging in every conceivable way. One morning Mom and I were discussing a devotion explaining how Jesus promises us an abundant life. It went on to read that the Greek term, 'perrison' means superabundant life. I asked mom what she pictures when she thinks about a superabundant life.

Her answer, "having the ability to handle anything that comes your way." That answer came from a believer who had to discern her juice from her oatmeal when asked to partake of one or the other. The God-sent affirmations found in His word and from other believers at such a time as this became the bread of life. The constant reminder of a presence extremely more powerful and useful than I could ever imagine or apply myself. The best advice is to not try and do things on your own. Seek God's counsel and pray without ceasing for everything you question. Know beyond a shadow of a doubt that when no one else is around and believe me that's going to happen, that the One who created you never leaves and remains a constant throughout your journey no matter what. Read scripture to your loved one. Allow them to hear God's words of encouragement and protection removing all feelings of abandonment if only for a moment. You'll realize that reading to them strengthens your relationship.

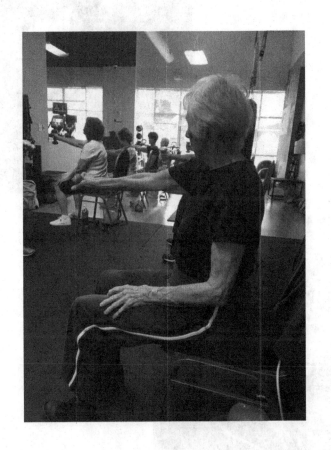

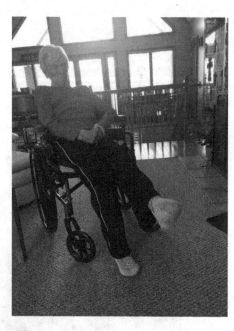

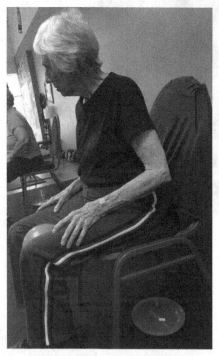

Verses to help:

Philippians 4:13 (NIV) - "I can do all this through Him who gives me strength."

1 Corinthians 3:16 (NIV) - "Don't you know that you yourselves are God's temple and that God's Spirit dwells in your midst?"

1 Corinthians 6:19 (NIV) – "Do you not know that your bodies are temples of the Holy Spirit, who is in you, whom you have received from God? You are not your own."

Proverbs 31:17 (NIV) - "She sets about her work vigorously; her arms are strong for her tasks."

1 Timothy 4:8 (NIV) - "For physical training is of some value, but godliness has value for all things, holding promise for both the present life and the life to come."

Joshua 14:11 (NIV) - "I am still as strong today as the day Moses sent me out; I'm just as vigorous to go out to battle now as I was then."

John 6:48 (NIV) - "I am the bread of life."

John 6:33 (NIV) - "For the bread of God is the bread that comes down from heaven and gives life to the world."

Proverbs 30:5 (NIV) - "Every word of God is flawless; He is a shield to those who take refuge in Him."

Romans 12:2 (NIV) - "Do not conform to the pattern of this world, but be transformed by the renewing of your mind. Then you will be able to test and approve what God's will is, His good, pleasing and perfect will."

1 Corinthians 1:25 (NIV) - "For the foolishness of God is wiser than human wisdom, and the weakness of God is stronger than human strength."

John 14:27 (NIV) - "Peace I leave with you; my peace I give you. I do not give to you as the world gives. Do not let your heart be troubled and do not be afraid."

Sundowners / Behaviors

I've heard and read about many who have shared the uncharacteristic behavior of their loved ones diagnosed with AD/Dementia. It's not uncommon to see this at all in your loved one. For example, although mom was the most caring, joy-filled individual with I know bad days every now and again, having the disease introduced us to whole new behaviors. Sundown syndrome is associated with increased confusion, agitation and restlessness. It's proposed that it happens more often in the evening hours because that time of day seems to be statistically when people are affected probably brought about by fatigue, depression, etc. It doesn't always have to be in the evenings as with mom. Many times it was but there were instances during the day we experienced it. It is not an easy task to face and fight and when it occurred at night, the result was a lack of sleep for all of us. There were many nights filled with hateful, fearful, and incomprehensible behaviors from mom. I remember calling my brothers asking them to speak with her hoping for some relief and resolve to the quandary we were in. Some evenings it worked, some evenings it soothed, and others, it ended being a stalemate. There were nights when those informal conversations with God and the adrenaline kicked in to get us through it. If my mother knew everything that had come from her mouth to one of us, it would have devastated her. Again, that's why Shiloh and I would always remind each other in our weakest moments that it was the disease. We knew it was never characteristic of her. Let me be clear, it did not mean we didn't take it personal at times or be hurt by it and by hurt, it would come knowing how it would have affected her had she truly known. It would always prove to be a test of patience. Did we always pass the tests? No, not all the time. There were indeed times I would try and divulge the demon as if I were performing an exorcism on her until I realized it was something I could not control. There were uncharacteristic traits we found quite surprising and amusing. One was mom consoling our dog, Levi. Mom was never an animal person. We had dogs growing up, but mom just existed and tolerated to please us. She was never the kind of person who would cuddle or be near the face of a dog or cat. Our German Shepherd, Levi, was diagnosed with osteosarcoma (bone cancer). He would always lie under mom's piano. He found comfort there, I guess. I had to step outside for a minute and upon returning, I walked in the house to witness something so astounding to me. Mom was lying next to Levi on the floor underneath her piano with her arm around him. Did she know? Did she sense his pain? It utterly amazed me. What I want you to realize and grasp is there will be horrific days and nights, but you must truly embrace the good, the pleasant, and the surprising behaviors you experience with your loved one. When you think about it, even in our own minds living with others, we all have good and bad days with the negatives always trying to diminish the positives. Do not let them. There are ways you can try and bring calm to your loved one when they are experiencing symptoms of Sundowners or just having a difficult day.

One thing I tried to keep consistent was a predictable routine when it came to bedtime, waking, and meals. There were times during preparing for bedtime that prolonged it. Her medication of sertraline seemed to assist with calming her during that time. Did it work every time? No, it did not and sometimes it would be like waiting for your baby to stop crying once you put her in her crib. Is it ever going to stop? I also had photographs, single and books, for her to look at. It did get to a point though that I had to intentionally introduce them to her to view. I also played music by a famous pianist, Anthony Burger, suggested to me and that seemed to soothe her or at least prompt her in that direction. Mom loved watching Andy Griffith and if they knew the future capabilities of that show back in the day, the awards would be flying, and Barney would be quite proud of himself at how he could bring a demon out of someone. Another calming for all of us was to just lie with each other whether it was watching Wheel of Fortune and Jeopardy enabling a team effort at playing, reading, or just in the quiet. This disease effect was a struggle for me. I indeed was tested many times and I found myself apologizing to Mom, to God, Shiloh, and to myself quite a bit. This element of the diseases knew how to push my buttons and gave me a continued growing hatred for them. I know I am human, but I would get so disappointed in myself for allowing the effects of a disease to invoke its behavior within me. I think it goes back to not being able to do anything about it or fix it, making me realize the need for surrender especially during those times.

Verses to help:

Ephesians 6:12 (NIV) - "For our struggle is not against flesh and blood but against the rulers, against the authorities, against the powers of this dark world and against the spiritual forces of evil in the heavenly realms."

2 Corinthians 10:4-5 (NIV) - "The weapons we fight with are not the weapons of the world. On the contrary, they have divine power to demolish strongholds. We demolish arguments and every pretension that sets itself up against the knowledge of God, and we take captive every thought to make it obedient to Christ."

Galatians 5:17 (NIV) - "For the flesh desires what is contrary to the Spirit, and the Spirit what is contrary to the flesh. They are in conflict with each other, so that you are not to do whatever you want."

Roman 8:7 (NIV) – The mind governed by the flesh is hostile to God; it does not submit to God's law, nor can it do so."

♪

Sundowners is a dreaded thing, it seems to take control
Creeping in to steal the joy embedded in her soul
A demon can appear at times in order to pick a fight
Leading to exhaustion from using strength and might
Embracing temporary as though soon it is to end
Witnessing the unusual is hard to comprehend
Its name gives time of day and while it may ring true
It may show up at other times, our hearts become so blue

♫

A demon it portrays coming from the mind
My mom who is in there but difficult to find
I know it isn't her, they locked her up somewhere
Trying to take control, it's difficult to bear
Reminded it's not her, diseases at their best
stealing from heart and soul, leaving us unrest

♪

They certainly do come out at night, Sundowners is a beast
Causing stress, anxiety and pain to say the least
It's like a monster, residing inside her mind
So unnatural, mean and surely enough unkind
How many nights must we endure, for her she knows not what
The agony, unlikeness, the sickness in my gut

♫

I'd get so agitated, defeat would cross my path
Giving in to the disease would surely be its wrath
I knew it wasn't her but at times it felt so wrong
disease would take her where she never did belong
At times I'd want to curse and tell it where to go
underneath my breath those thoughts would surely flow
But then I'd see her face and remember who she was
Holding and embracing exempting all the fuss
Don't let it overtake you somewhere to unknown fields
Trust in the process of love and wait upon its yields

♪

Always know their heart and from whence they came
To persevere throughout, the diseases without fame
Never make it a mountain, a hill only to climb
Look beyond yourself to get past this dreaded time
It will eventually pass and they will once again return
Show them love and honor, undoubtedly concern

Mystery

Alzheimer's and dementia are diseases that continuously remain mysteries. There's no true rhyme or reason for their existence and how they decide to feast on someone's brain. There's medications as we know to possibly treat the symptoms but as many differences in how the diseases affect everyone so that is with the medications. The brain shrinks enabling other organs to eventually shrink to shutting down. While I will let the professionals research the reasons behind the diseases, I will share the questions that continue to graze my brain where my mother was concerned. I know in part there's more to it than lifestyle. Mom was pure as the driven snow insofar as volunteering toxic additives to her body. I question the anesthesia from all the surgeries she had to undergo. I question whether or not it was the chemo and radiation she had to endure during her cancer journey. I question the food she ate, not that she didn't have a sensible diet or a well balanced one at that; or was it when they had to shock her heart multiple times during all her heart issues, depleting oxygen to her brain? Finally, I question the environment we live in. It is all a mystery! Why is it we can accept certain things as mysteries, acknowledging their presence but the mystery of having a God who loves us so much that He sent His only son to show us a better way of life is easily shoved aside as doubtful and unrealistic? In all of the early years to my adulthood being raised in church spending many a day in fellowship with other believers, I would question why God would love me that much. It's a mystery even still when you think about human nature and our inability to wrap our head around it or offer that same love. It's like when I was an Apparatus Operator in the Fire Service and I couldn't understand why I was to supply water, a certain psi, to the appliance connecting to the hose. I wanted to analyze it, a reason. They just said, "do it"! Why is it we have to be able to see something to believe it and not accept the effects of what it is we cannot see to believe the source from which it came? We can't see the wind but we sure can see the effects of the wind. It's all a mystery like the world of Alzheimer's and dementia. Except for the commonalities of memory loss and confusion, their effects differ in each individual they attach themselves to. I know without the dependence on our Creator and the ever-present example my mother set and kept during darkness, our journey could have ended in despair, greater hardships, and total loss. As much as I deplore the idea of giving gratitude to such horrible diseases, it became evident to me that no matter how hard they tried, it would never be powerful enough to evict the Holy Spirit from its residence inside mom's heart and soul. It certainly strengthened my faith and will forever be ingrained in me that throughout our journey, mom not once forgot who Jesus was, her best friend, even when she would forget who we were. It is all a mystery!

Verses to help:

Ecclesiastes 11:5 (NIV) - "As you do not know the path of the wind, or how the body is formed in a mother's womb, so you cannot understand the work of God, the Maker of all things."

1 Corinthians 2:7 (NIV) - "No, we declare God's wisdom, a mystery that has been hidden and that God destined for our glory before time began."

Job 11:7 (NIV) - "Can you fathom the mysteries of God? Can you probe the limits of the Almighty?"

Ephesians 1:9 (NIV) - "He made known to us the mystery of His will according to his good pleasure, which he purposed in Christ."

Ephesians 3:4 (NIV) - "In reading this, then, you will be able to understand my insight into the mystery of Christ."

Colossians 1:27 (NIV) - "To them God has chosen to make known among the Gentiles the glorious riches of this mystery, which is Christ in you, the hope of glory."

Isaiah 46:4 (NIV) - "Even to your old age and gray hairs I am He, I am He who will sustain you I have made you and I will carry you; I will sustain you and I will rescue you."

Late Stage / Transition

I don't think any amount of time, experience, or anticipated outcome can prepare you for the transition of your loved one. When it comes to an end-of-life phase of any disease, it becomes such an emotional roller-coaster. You do not desire them to leave this earth. You do not desire them to suffer. You know life has been difficult, yet you have withstood the test of time. You do not want to over medicate them because you want them to know they are not alone. With the diseases of Alzheimer's and dementia, it begins with the shrinkage of the brain making way to other bodily functions or organs shutting down until their last breath. Witnessing first-hand your loved one going from a vibrant, independent person to a person losing all capabilities of any task is by far one of the most disheartening experiences I have ever encountered. I have seen a lot throughout my years in my profession of firefighting. It seems though that while you are living it, you do not have the time to dwell on the differences. You continue to do what you can to make them comfortable. The love never ceases. I was not looking forward to this time even though I knew I wanted peace for mom. Honestly, there would be days I would wonder how it would be not to be in the position we were in. I learned that the expected is not always expected even knowing the consequences of the disease. We were caregivers in the midst of the COVID pandemic. Shiloh and I both contracted COVID in December of 2020 while being caregivers for mom. We were being so careful and I'm not quite sure how it ended up entering our household and I can only speculate it was a nurse who had been there a couple of days earlier bringing us supplies. She had tested positive. Nevertheless, it became another obstacle while and in caring for mom. The blame that came upon myself for having the virus and laying with mom not realizing I had it became something I had to work through. I would soon be wearing a mask while doing what needed to be done having to be close to mom at this point, physically picking her up and assisting with other cognitive dysfunctions. COVID took so much from me. I would find myself continuing to care for my family only to retreat to the basement finding any moment to rest pleading to God to get me through it. Mom was in the latter stages of the disease and I knew her breathing was becoming more difficult; plus, with the idleness that was taking place came the opportunity for pneumonia to set in and I could not help but wonder if she had the virus as well. The way it spread, how could she not? At that point, people were dying and there was no manifestation of treatments. The virus was new, and testing was offsite and no in-home testing available. I had to continue caring for her at this juncture of our journey. It became more evident with her labored breathing and inability to rise, our journey was becoming more of a reality. Again, not necessarily expected, but a different path. The routine became turning her body to keep sores at bay, feeding her the only way I could with liquids until that would no longer sustain. In many ways two weeks would seem like two years and in others, they flew by because of the constant care. I know mom believed to Whom she belonged and what would be waiting for her but she had such a will to live on this planet earth. She loved people. She loved her family fiercely and the experience we were encountering made me feel as if she wanted to hang on to this life. Then, on January 17, 2021, I sensed she was in the beginning phases of her transition from this earth. Shiloh and I rallied and laid with her singing songs she would sing to us when we were both younger, like "Everything's Okay in My Father's House". I phoned Hosparus to let them know about the development and questioned the amount of medicine to administer to her to keep her from experiencing pain. I administered one small dose of what was given in the packet we received and we continued to lie with her. She did not seem to focus on anything, just trying to get her breath until I had to walk away for a split second and when Shiloh stepped in my place and took her hand, mom's eyes were open and completely focused on her. Shiloh then 15, said to her, "Grand mommy, everything is going to be okay. It's okay Grand mommy, it's all going to be okay." At that moment, we both witnessed mom taking her last two breaths and it was all so surreal. I have played that experience in my head more times than I want to admit. It was difficult but meaningful knowing Shiloh played such a huge role in her transition serving as another reminder of her existence, knowing my mother and I needed that guidance and support at such a time as then. I then called my brothers to let them know along with Hosparus. Hosparus in turn contacted the funeral home who made arrangements to pick her body up to transport her to their location. I found it terribly difficult seeing them take her away. There was a part of me that did not want them to. They were very comforting allowing our time with her. It was a cold blustering night and I wanted them to keep her safe. I know it sounds silly knowing her body and soul were finally at peace. I did contact those who I felt would want to know rather than wait. I found myself from the time she left the house and days after, sitting and questioning what in the world I was supposed to do. I had my daughter to continue caring for but this was something even she had grown accustomed to. What were we going to do? It would take days, even months to forge into a new norm and routine. We miss her terribly and wherever we are, we always try to find something to remind us of her presence. There's times things just show up, like on vacation and seeing her name on a license plate, etc. As my nephew Elijah so eloquently shared at her memorial service, there's a piece of grandmother in each of us to carry her legacy, her love, and faith forward. Grief is not a one-time event. It follows you wherever you go, whatever you're doing and will show up at the most inopportune time. The length of time to navigate that grief is unlimited and different for everyone. It's been two and a half years since mom made her transition and I still have yet to clean out her closet. What I've come to realize is that if there were no grief, there would be no love. It's during those times when grief makes its appearance that I remind myself of the love that existed between a mother, a daughter, and a granddaughter and having the faith in that "one more" resurrects a hope that is beyond all understanding.

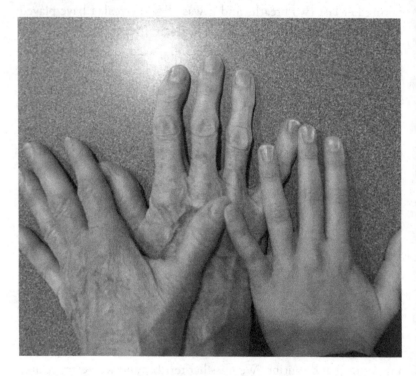

Verses to help:

Psalm 71:20 (NIV) - "Though you have made me see troubles, many and bitter, you will restore my life again; from the depths of the earth you will again bring me up."

Psalm 73:26 (NIV) – "My flesh and my heart may fail, but God is the strength of my heart and my portion forever."

2 Corinthians 4:16-18 (NIV) - "Therefore we do not lose heart. Though outwardly we are wasting away, yet inwardly we are being renewed day by day. For our light and momentary troubles are achieving for us an eternal glory that far outweighs them all. So, we fix our eyes not on what is seen, but on what is unseen, since what is seen is temporary, but what is unseen is eternal."

Psalm 39:4 (NIV) - "Show me, Lord, my life's end and the number of my days; let me know how fleeting my life is."

Daniel 12:13 (NIV) - "As for you, go your way till the end. You will rest, and then at the end of the days you will rise to receive your allotted inheritance."

John 6:63 (NIV) - "The Spirit gives life; the flesh counts for nothing. The words I have spoken to you – they are full of the Spirit and life."

Psalm 36:9 (NIV) - "For with you is the fountain of life; in your light we see light."

Ecclesiastes 7:1 (NIV) - "A good name is better than precious ointment; and the day of death than the day of one's birth."

1 Corinthians 15:55 (NIV) - "Where O death, is your victory? Where, O death, is your sting? The sting of death is sin, and the power of sin is the law. But thanks be to God! He gives us the victory through our Lord Jesus Christ."

Psalm 23 (NIV) - "The Lord is my Shepherd, I shall not want. He maketh me to lie down in green pastures; He leadeth me beside the still waters, He restoreth my soul; He leadeth me in the paths of righteousness for his name's sake. Yea, though I walk through the valley of the shadow of death, I will fear no evil; for thou are with me; Thy rod and thy staff they comfort me. Thou preparest a table before me in the presence of mine enemies; Thou anointest my head with oil; my cup runneth over. Surely goodness and mercy shall follow me all the days of my life; and I will dwell in the house of the Lord forever."

Matthew 5:4 (NIV) - "Blessed are those who mourn, for they will be comforted."

2 Corinthians 1:4 (NIV) - "Praise be to the God and Father of our Lord Jesus Christ, the Father of compassion and the God of all comfort, who comforts us in all our troubles, so that we can comfort those in any trouble with the comfort we ourselves receive from God."

Matthew 5:8 (NIV) - "Blessed are the pure in heart, for they will see God."

♪

Eight Years

Diagnosis came eight years ago, it seems it's been terribly long
Changes made throughout her life have felt many times so wrong
I've managed to collect my thoughts and accept the ones that came
Now she's losing so much weight, my heart feels so much shame
Part of the disease they say, there's nothing you can do
Milk shakes in an IV? Something she didn't have to chew?
Even when you feed her, she simply will say "enough"!
Do you impose your will or politely accept the slough?
Oh, Alzheimer's, how will your demise play out?
The fight we have within, for us it leaves no doubt

♫

Near The End

She's asking, "what's happened"? I feel she knows it's near
I pray to God to show He's close, to take away her fear
I told her she's always been my best friend, you see
First of all she was the greatest mother she could be
Her love deserves the best with loved ones all around
Teaching us to know where love is surely found
A believer she's always been, a fan of Jesus, not only so
She's walked the walk and followed Him wherever she would go

♥

Does She Know?

Does she know how much she's loved when at times love was so tough?
Does she know each person touched and how it was enough?
Does she know that even though we veered from what she taught
that foundation which was laid was something can't be bought?
Does she know the imprint made while loving as they are
Didn't matter who they were, those from home or from afar
Does she know the impact on the little minds she served
And how they grew to remember her with love and not unnerve
Does she know that every key played was beautiful at least
Music was a way for her to share an abundant feast
Does she know the smile she has lights up more than a room
And how without a word creates joy in place of gloom
Oh God, please help her know what she means to a mass
Whether meeting them or not, they know she is first class
When you truly think about it, she probably knows not much
Humility of her gifts of love, her heart, her soul as such

Year of Her Passing....

This past year has been so difficult, to some would find relief
All the days leading up to it would ne'er pass up the grief
All year long, pictures have appeared before my eyes
The traits you incurred, one gets before one dies
Some say we'll meet again and I will come to you
I feel your presence with me in many things I do
When putting on my make-up, suddenly you'll appear
I see and feel you placing yours as though you are so near
Deodorant, another, the movement back and forth
I feel you through my movement when moving south to north
And then there are the teeth, loyal up until the end
Dementia added to the length of strokes that you would fend
When I say no news to read or see for me today
I'm reminded of your words, "it lets me know how to pray".
I'm missing being "auntie" in the mornings as we would chat
The presence that I felt from her helped me get through all that
Our days and nights were challenging to say the least at times
Your absence from this present world caches all those whines
The constant love of people you exhibited to me
Left me such big shoes to fill, I think many would agree
I just know since you've left this earth, regrets for me, no, none
Your goodness and your grace are missed when all is said and done

♪

With the holidays approaching, the lights seem oh, so dim
Realities of your absence, changing emotions on a whim
The first one is most difficult or so they seem to say
Continuing hopefulness and getting by day by day
Attempting to uphold traditions, preparing things your way
You, the rock, the matriarch, they just don't seem to stay
Life just seems so different now, we know it to be true
Lacking your physical presence leaves me oh, so blue
May we not lose sight of just who you really were
while living on this earth, may it not end up a blur
Finding extensions of you, you see, within our own heart
Despite all of the frailties, that intend to keep us apart
May the unconditional love to us, you so graciously gave
Remind us of our family and what's so needed to save
You may not be with us, but I can still hear you chuckle
Thirty minutes past the joke, belts needing to unbuckle
Your desire to live despite difficulties that enveloped you so
has me contemplating my own life and how I need to grow
May we all be reminded that life is but a mist
The physical nature on this earth temporarily exist
And so, the truth be told, the spirit does compel
Our hearts and our minds, thou we know must dwell

Resources

There are many resources to assist in navigating the journey of Alzheimer's and dementia. Initially I was blessed with knowing Dr. Benjamin Mast, a psychologist specializing in aging and the diseases. I read his book entitled "The Second Forgetting, Remembering the Power of the Gospel during Alzheimer's disease." This book reiterated that no matter how the diseases attempt to destroy us and our relationships, God is ever present walking and carrying us through our journey. Words he spoke into me during one of our encounters was "Roxanne, you know what's better for your mom than what she knows at this time." This statement was forever branded in my heart and mind and assisted me in making whatever decisions I had to make without feeling guilty or selfish. It's true you know? After a while they don't have the mental capability to make sound decisions and you have to do that for them. There are also scheduled meetings held at the Alzheimer's Association in whatever city you may live in. I attended the Alzheimer's Association of Louisville a few times. It allowed me to meet others who were traveling the same road. I will never forget meeting an older couple and while watching them I realized the disease had taken her voice. Her husband and caregiver so graciously made sure she was taken care of. I could sense the love between the two of them, much like I witnessed in the movie, "The Notebook". With them, there was no need for verbal communication and I deeply appreciated his kindness toward her. To me that spoke volumes. This particular meeting's agenda was to provide the attendees with an education on medications, their interactions, measuring effect between drug burden and function, adverse drug reactions, drug trials, etc. with the presentation given by a University of Louisville Doctor of Pharmacy, Department of Family Medicine and Geriatrics. She presented us with a multifaceted overview of medications, side effects of many, how they relate to a diagnosed target and how in turn they may be counter intuitive. I also learned how medication affects those with Alzheimer's and/or dementia and the elderly. I believe the workshop assisted me in navigating mom's medications alongside her doctor as I shared in our Medication experience. The Alzheimer's Association has a website that includes various information pertaining to help, support and research with the encouragement of getting involved in your local chapter. "Myalzteam" is a social network having a member stories blog where you may share your own experiences and learn from others. There are also support groups held at specific locations, hospitals, churches, etc. who provide much needed emotional support. It seemed for me like that of the Fire Service, I would listen to others and while our experience was indeed horrendous at times, someone else would always have it worse. A friend of mine who was also a caregiver for her mother created a reader-supported publication entitled "Keeping It Real Caregiving" and the goal is to share news, information, and guidance from real caregivers which can also assist you in your journey. I also have a longtime friend who was also in the midst of caring for her mother, although different circumstances, it allowed us to vent, laugh and share tactics in caregiving. Laughter is always resourceful!

The Veteran's Association contributed to the ability of taking mom to the Adult Day centers. Since my dad had been a veteran, even though deceased, they were able to help some financially toward the cost. It did not cover all the days she attended but every little bit helped. There seemed to be a lot of paperwork and red tape to go through for verification and you could get overwhelmed by it all but it's worth it to try and receive the help needed. I know there are other books out there as well that have a story to tell and while they may be different from your own personal experience, it may bring comfort to you knowing you're not alone. As shared previously, there are nursing facilities that provide temporary stays for loved ones when respite becomes a necessity for going out of town, vacationing, etc. I inquired about the possibility but never utilized them for personal reasons. While I wasn't a frequent recipient to what was provided for multiple reasons, some of which included work, continued care for mom and my family and the fact I was in the midst of it all, I found comfort in sharing our story on social media. I knew there were so many people who loved mom and were concerned for her and our journey. This was an avenue of opportunity to share with our friends and family how the diseases affected mom and all of us. The comfort I felt knowing there were those among us, near and far, who were embracing us with prayer and petition and supporting us with their love was more than I could ever ask for. Journaling and poetry are also other avenues to escape even though you may be writing about your life as it is. There is something about getting things off your chest through a pen or pencil and even a computer. It then becomes a treasure when you can look back and read about what you yourself survived through the grace of God in loving and assisting your loved one. You could also reach out to family members and friends, creating a list of dates and times they could visit or even phone your loved one. Many people think once memory loss reaches a certain point there is no need to communicate because they no longer know who they are or can communicate in the way they are comfortable with. They may feel their time is too valuable. It is our responsibility to reiterate the moments of joy. They will receive a blessing as well. Another organization who many fear and tend to define as an end-of-life alternative is Hosparus. Hosparus of Indiana where we live, in the mid to latter stages became an appreciated and valuable resource. While I continued to check mom's vitals alongside normal care, they would send a nurse to check in on her and bring us any supplies we needed like undergarments, bed sheet protectors, and always a smile.

We were also given an end-of-life medication packet that stayed on our refrigerator shelf for quite some time and was only used a couple of times to bring calm and when mom was about to make her transition. They also took over ordering the medications for mom and provided a Chaplain who would visit us every couple of weeks to pray and talk with us, individually and together. Our chaplain became such a blessing, and it was reciprocated when she became quite enamored with mom and the Holy Spirit's dwelling within her. As Christians, we are told in order to experience growth in our relationship with Christ, we need to nurture that relationship as with any. God's word is a recipe for life no matter what circumstances you find yourself in, i.e. the scripture shared in this book pertaining to our journey. You'll always find encouragement and direction.

Verses to help:

2 Corinthians 9:12 (NIV) - "This service that you perform is not only supplying the needs of the Lord's people but is also overflowing in many expressions of thanks to God."

Philippians 2:4 (NIV) – "not looking to your own interests but each of you to the interests of the others."

Galatians 6:2 (NIV) - "Carry each other's burdens, and in this way you will fulfill the law of Christ."

Isaiah 41:6 (NIV) - "They help each other and say to their companions, "Be strong!""

Ecclesiastes 4:10 (NIV) - "if either of them falls down one can help the other up. But pity anyone who falls and has no one to help them up."

Philippians 4:19 (NIV) - "And my God will meet all your needs according to the riches of his glory in Christ Jesus."

Summary

We were informed from the beginning of time that in this life we would have an array of troubles, hardships and sufferings of all kind. Although we respond many times in the midst as if we can't see that or think certain things couldn't happen to us or unthought of circumstances delivered to us, the reality of the truth is what it is. This challenging fire of the journey of Alzheimer's and dementia along with many others I've traveled provided more lessons than I could have ever imagined. It's difficult to see them in the midst but as David shares in Psalm 23, **"God guides me along the right paths for his name's sake, and even though I walk through the darkest valley, I will fear no evil, for you are with me...".** I was my mother's primary caregiver. I was caring for her, it would seem. God in his infinite wisdom used my mother to continue teaching me as she always did. Little did I realize earlier while surrounded by chaos, how impactful those lessons would become. Being able to remember the name of and relationship with **Jesus** in the midst of forgetting everything else substantiated the existence of His presence in the lives of those who love Him and that He's not just another name. I was also reminded of looking at life by the moments accepting how my mother dealt with it and honestly, a proper way to live, taking nothing for granted and embracing those moments like the joy she would get the moment she received a visit or a phone call if only seconds later, memory loss would get the best of her. There's purpose, also having its place since the beginning of time, and the realization of the need to instill it in those who have forgotten or seem to lose theirs in the journey. My communication skills were honed during this time through trial and error of course so that I could better understand the effects of the disease and what my mother was going through although difficult at times. The diseases show us how they may try to steal much from those afflicted with them and even ourselves but they can never take away the love we have for one another, nor the love God has for all of us. There is also the reiteration of positives in everything as much as the enemy tries to erase them and our responsibility to forge ahead embracing them in the midst of our adversaries. An attitude of gratitude is not just a holiday expression but an ingredient in the recipe of life. The sanctification received during this journey undoubtedly leaves no room for regrets. I value and hold on to the moments of clarity where in the beginning the difficulties of transition were later swapped with the words of "thank you sis, I don't know what I would do without you."

Thank You, Lord.

I hope and pray you feel love in these words and know in writing them provided a peace beyond measure for me. Healing comes in many forms. I thank God for using mom throughout her life to bless others especially during a vulnerable and challenging time. I thank God for supplying all my needs. May God bless and keep you as you witness or become directly involved with any infirmities that come your way. Acknowledge Him and your paths will be directed.